BRITAIN'S
LOST CHURCHES

BRITAIN'S LOST CHURCHES

~

THE FORGOTTEN HOLY SITES
OF BRITAIN'S CHRISTIAN PAST

MATTHEW HYDE

First published in Great Britain
2015 by Aurum Press Ltd
74–77 White Lion Street
Islington
London N1 9PF
www.aurumpress.co.uk

A catalogue record for this book is available from the British Library.

ISBN 978 1 78131 121 9

10 9 8 7 6 5 4 3 2 1
2019 2018 2017 2016 2015

Layout by Joanna MacGregor
Printed in China

Previous page: *The Booton angels.*
This page: *Elgin, the lost Lanthorn of the north.*
Next page: *Coventry Cathedral after the Blitz of November 1940.*

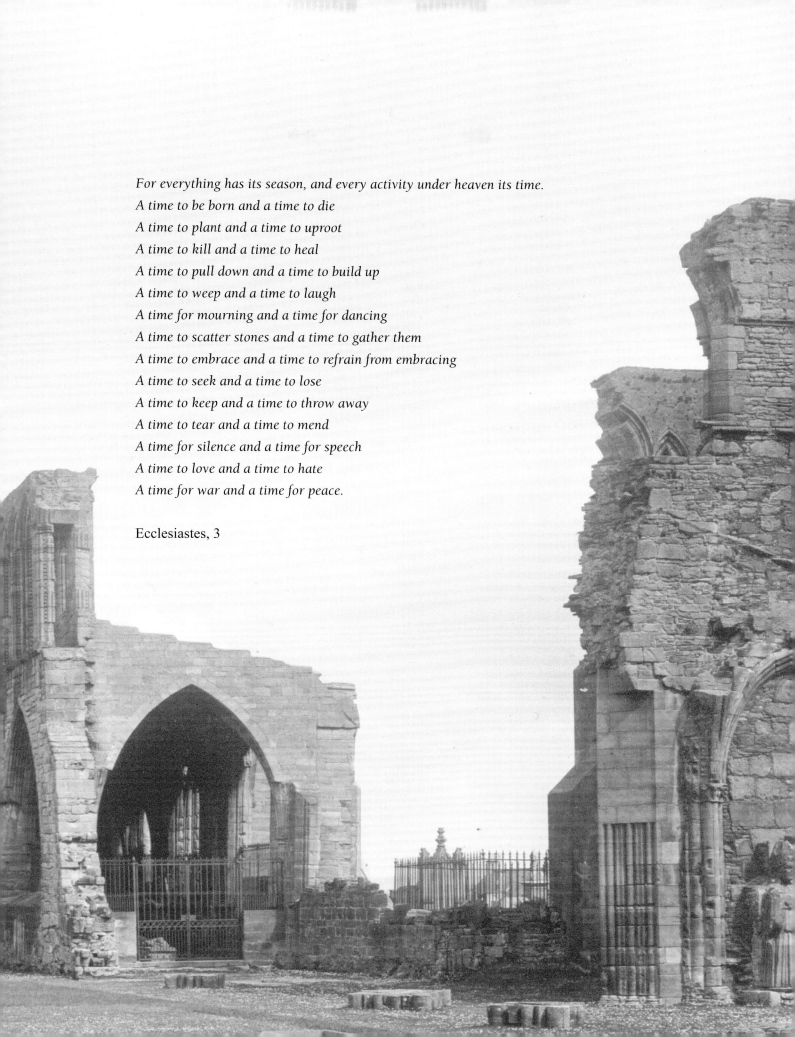

For everything has its season, and every activity under heaven its time.
A time to be born and a time to die
A time to plant and a time to uproot
A time to kill and a time to heal
A time to pull down and a time to build up
A time to weep and a time to laugh
A time for mourning and a time for dancing
A time to scatter stones and a time to gather them
A time to embrace and a time to refrain from embracing
A time to seek and a time to lose
A time to keep and a time to throw away
A time to tear and a time to mend
A time for silence and a time for speech
A time to love and a time to hate
A time for war and a time for peace.

Ecclesiastes, 3

CONTENTS

PROLOGUE

❧

The scene: a hippy wedding in 1968, captured in a photograph in the slightly garish colour of the time. The bride wears a very short dress of untraditional orange, the groom a kipper tie and flared trousers. Both are absurdly young. The setting: the Catholic church of St George, Kettlethorpe, near Wakefield, a brick building of 1957 with an internal frame of laminated wood. The newly married couple stand, awkward but happy, in front of the church door. The background: cracked concrete paving, a patch of worn grass and distant council houses. Nearby stands the giant Crigglestone Colliery, the major local employer, with its winding gear, sidings and dirt rucks.

Thirty years later, visiting old haunts, the couple, now grown respectable, seek out St George's, Kettlethorpe, only to find that the church has gone. There is no evidence that it has ever existed, save only the name applied to a group of new houses: St George's Mews. Astonishingly there is no sign of the colliery either; it has vanished without a trace, the site greened over, its very name expunged.

▶ *Right: Walberswick, a church mostly ruined, like Coverhithe, nearby.*

In Memory of
ELIZABETH the loving Wife of
THOMAS TROTTER who
departed this Life March
20th 1781
Aged 57 Years

O Cruel Death who was so unkind was thee
The best and dearest Friend to take from me
The sole joy and comfort of my Life
A tender Mother and a loving Wife

INTRODUCTION

~

In about the year 1003, in the shock of relief that the first millennium had not seen the end of the world, a monk called Rodolphus Glaber, or Ralph the Bald, was able to look with satisfaction into the future, rejoicing that all Europe was cladding itself in 'a white mantle of churches'. The phrase has stuck. He was writing at the Burgundian abbey of Cluny in eastern central France, which was itself expanding at a prodigious rate and would end up as one of the greatest of all medieval monasteries, surrounded by a multitude of lesser churches. Churches at the time were often literally white, too, coated from top to bottom with gleaming lime wash. Traces of lime wash can be seen at Elmham, for instance (see chapter 7), or on the early Norman masonry of Cubley in Derbyshire; Wordsworth's evocation of Hawkshead, 'I saw the snow-white church upon her hill', recalls the annual lime-washing which was still then customary. We can get an impression of a mantle of churches if we look out from a church tower in Norfolk, where other church towers can be seen in all directions. Even now a random stroll through the City of London seems to reveal a little white church steeple set between the bankers' towers at every corner. In this case it is the Portland stone which confers their whiteness; the magnificent photographs of George Birch show how fine the views were before the Blitz, when half a dozen were lost (many more disappeared in the late nineteenth century) and when the surrounding buildings were still dwarfed by the church steeples.

An observer in about 1500 might have felt even greater satisfaction at the apparent vigour and richness of the Church, the hundreds of monastic foundations that had tamed the wilderness and offered care and education in the community, and the thousands of parish churches that were the centre of village and town life. Much church building was still going on in the parishes and monasteries. It was the age of magnificent towers and of huge windows needed to accommodate stained glass.

Just thirty years later it was all to be swept away. The matrimonial difficulties of Henry VIII were the catalyst, leading to a breakaway from Rome. In a mere ten years Henry's greed and the gathering strength of the Reformation had led to the abolition of every monastery in England and Wales, the destruction of their fabric and the confiscation of their wealth. Many have been left as ruins, which may, like Tintern or Rievaulx, be considered beautiful in their own right, but others have disappeared almost completely. Sometimes a single surviving piece, such as the statuesque St Christopher at Norton Priory near Runcorn, gives a clue to how much has been lost. A most delicate yet vigorous depiction of a Christ figure wrestling with a lion carved on vaulting boss is almost all that is left at Hailes in

St Michael in the marketplace,
Macclesfield.

Gloucestershire. The superb Syon cope, now in the Victoria & Albert Museum, is another example (see chapter 2).

Scotland's reformation took longer but was even more severe in the end, and even Cluny, from where Ralph the Bald made his earlier observations, was lost in the French Revolution of 1790, leaving just a fragment of its former splendour.

A century of religious upheaval was to follow, leaving parish churches and parish life stripped of all colour and imagery, shorn of the religious and social feasts which had enlivened the medieval year, and with a greatly simplified liturgy in English rather than Latin. It is surprising that they survived at all, especially as independent chapels were now springing up in every corner of the land.

Stability was at last achieved in the long Georgian age which stretched the century until about 1830, but it was hardly vigorous. The parson was a distant figure; congregations dozed. The appeal of John Wesley's emotional message of personal salvation is understandable, especially when voiced by his brother Charles's uplifting hymns. Georgian architecture was as rational and well mannered as the estate church of Normanton in Rutland, although that has

had an extraordinary and romantic recent history (see chapter 4). In any case, behind the apparent rationality of John Wood's architecture at Bath and at his lost Llandaff Cathedral (see chapter 7) lay some pretty wild theories.

Then followed a second great resurgence as the Victorians re-sanctified (as they saw it) the Church, reinventing the Gothic style and reinstating stained glass, encaustic tiles, mosaic and even wall painting. The liturgy was enriched and became more ceremonious. It was another huge change and it did not please everyone. This is when the distinctions arose between 'High' and 'Low' in churchmanship, which could have dire consequences, as examined in chapter 5. Nonconformists were not immune, often chiming with a new Gothic building in front of the old chapel, or with a florid building in classical style, as at Cleckheaton and Heckmondwike in Yorkshire (see chapter 8). The revived work was always unmistakably Victorian, though. However much you may hanker after a lost golden age it can never truly be resurrected. Indeed, attempts to restore an old church to its former glory could, ironically, result in greater destruction than if it were left alone. The architect George Gilbert Scott was accused of falsifying the past in his restorations at Chester (see page 15), Nantwich and Stafford and no doubt many other places, as was Lord Grimthorpe at St Alban's. The Shell Guides, among other such publications, often excoriate Victorian 'scraping', and yet Victorian interventions often saved a church that would otherwise have collapsed – as at Stafford.

A second holocaust was visited upon the country in the Blitz of 1940–41. Aerial attacks were concentrated upon Britain's cities although stray bombs could

This page: Rhuddlan Castle, North Wales.

land almost anywhere, as they did in Bunbury in Cheshire in November 1940, and Chilvers Coton in May 1941 (see chapter 9). The peace that followed often saw them rise again, as at Coventry, and sometimes greater than before. Many, however, have stayed lost, such as Christchurch Newgate Street in the City of London or Charles Church in Plymouth.

The second millennium was again accompanied by prophecies of doom, although this time it was a virtual doom as the breakdown of computer systems was predicted. The year 2000 found churches and chapels of every description in decline. A steep decline in the case of Methodism in Wales and Cornwall, for example; a slow slide with the advancing age of congregations in the Church of England and its equivalents in Wales and Scotland, affected by scandals and lack of vocations in the Catholic Church.

Churches and chapels are being lost today not through religious strife or war but through declining attendance and consequent insufficient finances. Doctrinal change will sometimes condemn a church, as at Cardross (see chapter 10), and catastrophe such as the Great Fire of 1666 which destroyed old St Paul's, or the lightning which nearly destroyed York Minster in 1984, can strike any time. However, a fire can sometimes reveal a church that was thought lost, as happened in 1834 with St Stephen's in Westminster (see chapter 3). In general, we are seeing a slow attrition, particularly tragic in the case of the Brigittines of Syon who have survived so much (see chapter 2).

Does it matter? Church and chapel can no longer be said to be central to national life, and the fabric of society has not collapsed yet, so why should we care? Memories of travel in communist Eastern Europe in the 1960s can provide some answers. An abiding image of a trip I took through Russia in 1966 was the village with its cluster of gingerbread wooden houses and at its centre the church, its onion dome split open, walls collapsing. It was as though the heart of the community had been torn out. In Prague in 1968 it was almost impossible among all those spires and domes to find a single functioning church on a Sunday, though the Maltese church in Mala Strana did in the end provide a somewhat clandestine mass. Here in Britain it was a shock to find that the principal old church in the centre of Shrewsbury, St Mary, had been abandoned by its congregation and vested in the Churches Conservation Trust. Today in Eastern Europe the clock has been turned back: Orthodox services are crowded, and long lost churches such as St Michael of the Golden Domes in Kiev have risen again on their old foundations.

Where a church has been lost through enemy action or violent cultural change there is often a determination that the aggressor should not win and to bring back what has been lost. Loss through decline is more difficult to reverse but it can most certainly be done, simply with the arrival of a new vicar or minister, with a revamping of the building, or with diversification and the discovery of a new purpose. Building work at a church in 2014 is likely to involve the provision of toilets and a kitchen, sometimes even part conversion into a café, shop, post office or library, so that the place is versatile and can be kept open and welcoming every day. It may be that such creeping secularisation is a sort of loss, but then so is a permanently locked door or death through inertia.

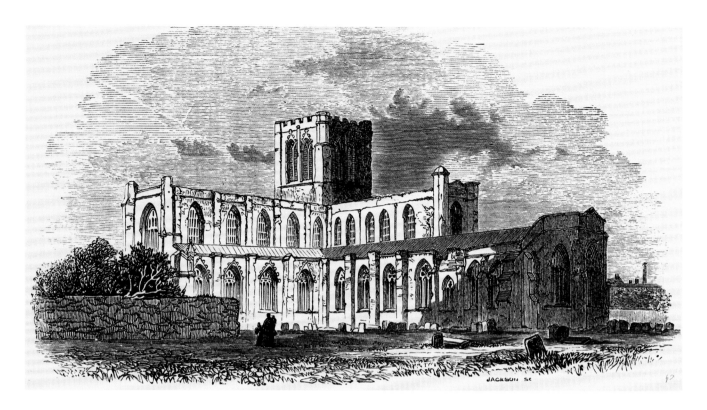

A ROYAL PROGRESS, 1278

It is very rare that we can know the whereabouts of a particular figure from long ago on a particular day. In the case of the formidable King Edward I and his beloved queen, Eleanor of Castile, however, the royal records provide a day-to-day itinerary (they usually travelled together, even on campaign), enabling us to reconstruct the different scenes with some accuracy. The royal progress for a single year, 1278, illustrates the different ways in which a church may become lost.

△ **Above**: *Chester Cathedral from the south east before the drastic restorations of the nineteenth century.*

In March the royal party was in Glastonbury over Easter for a great and solemn occasion, the reburial of King Arthur and Queen Guinevere. The king himself bore the bones of his illustrious – nay, mythical – ancestor to the new grave, as likewise, did Eleanor. It was an occasion freighted with symbolism which cemented the drawing power of what was already one of the richest abbeys in the land. Equally great was to be its fall, as is recounted in chapter 2.

In May and June the royal party was at Westminster for parliament. Edward was even then contemplating the building of a royal chapel, St Stephen, to rival La Sainte Chapelle in Paris whose consecration his father Henry III had witnessed. The surprising story of that chapel is told in chapter 2.

Edward, accompanied as always by Eleanor, was at Rhuddlan in North Wales from 7 to 12 September, where his state-of-the-art castle was under construction. The sister castle and the planned town of Flint were being built at the same time. The astounding castles of Conwy, Harlech, Caernarfon and, finally, Beaumaris were soon to follow.

When in 1282 the ancient cathedral of St Asaph was in the midst of the fighting, fired by English soldiers under the Earl of Warwick in order to prevent it from harbouring the enemy, Edward wanted the cathedral transferred to his new fortified town of Rhuddlan. In the event it was reconstructed on its old site.

The border city of Chester was Edward's great entrepôt, where he gathered everything he needed for his Welsh campaigns: the armies, the ships, the supplies, armourers, coiners, and the finest master masons and engineers in all Christendom. For a while, therefore, Cheshire and North Wales were at the cutting edge of culture and technology.

In the winter, and in times of truce, attention could be turned from war to more peaceful enterprises. In Chester itself the great Benedictine abbey church of St Werburgh, today the cathedral, was being rebuilt stage by stage. The beautiful Lady Chapel was finished in about 1280, then the choir was rebuilt to a new design, bay by bay. The work progressed in fits and starts because the masons might be called way at a moment's notice, and it is visibly disjointed as a result.

Passing through Chester, the royal party – it should be remembered that in the king's retinue was a veritable army of about six hundred – travelled on to Vale Royal in mid-Cheshire, where it arrived on 24 September. The king wished to see the progress of his works on his great abbey which had been consecrated in his presence the previous year. A Cistercian foundation, Vale Royal had been founded by Edward in 1270 as the consequence of a vow made during a perilous sea voyage. It was planned on a truly royal scale, intended to outshine all others

▲ **Above**: *From the south-east, Chester Cathedral after restoration and reconstruction by Scott and others.*

▶ **Opposite page left**: *A Victorian painting of Macclesfield St Michael in its 1744 incarnation.*

▶ **Opposite page right**: *The same view a century or so later, after a near-complete rebuild by Blomfield in 1899–1901.*

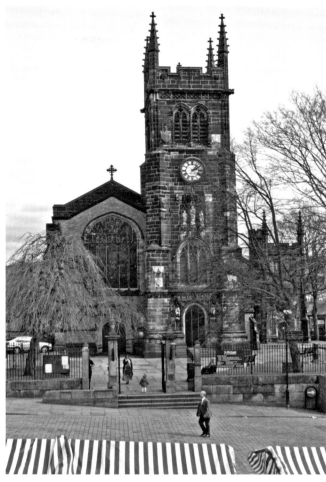

in size and magnificence.

The royal progress continued to the east Cheshire town of Macclesfield, where, from 1 to 3 October 1278 the Queen of all England, Eleanor of Castile, witnessed the consecration of her church of All Hallows (today St Michael and All Angels) by the Bishop of St Asaph. The king was at her side but it was Eleanor's affair, for the church, manor and forest of Macclesfield were in her own possession. As the celebrants moved around the building each stage in the ceremony was marked by a consecration cross inscribed on the stonework. At least one of these survives, on the jamb of the south door.

A modern and unroyal progress in the reverse direction will show how these foundations have fared over the intervening centuries.

Of Queen Eleanor's church in Macclesfield there is at first sight little evidence. The church in

the marketplace, at the top of the 108 steps that climb up from the River Bollin, is apparently late Victorian. It turns out that Eleanor's church has been lost not once, but twice. The first time was in 1744, a time of rapid growth in the town. Her entire church was demolished excepting only the tower and the sixteenth-century Savage Chapel, and then rebuilt as a galleried preaching box. By taking a step to the north it was made much bigger than the old one. One hundred and fifty years later, however, the Victorians evidently considered this style of church inappropriate and unworshipful, so the Georgian church was taken down in its turn in 1899–1901 and rebuilt in a more 'correct' Gothic style. Even now, however, the arms of Castile are displayed over the west door.

A close examination of the fabric shows that a good deal more of Eleanor's church survives than has generally been supposed. Under the Victorian skin the tower is entirely medieval. The top stage was added in the 1470s, but the lower three stages belong to Eleanor's church. It may have had a spire, too. The tall tower arch and a fine tierceron vault give an idea of the quality of its court style in a county where the humbler churches were generally of wood, and the height of the tower arch gives us the height of her lost church. The responds of the lost arcades indicate the width of the nave – it was quite narrow in relation to its height – and the south door the width of the aisles.

Edward's great abbey of Vale Royal has come to naught. It is truly lost, bar a few elaborately moulded stones placed on the site of the high altar and now marooned on the practice green of a golf course. It is almost impossible to imagine the scene on 2 August 1277 when Edward laid a foundation stone on this very spot.

When the monastery was dissolved in 1538 the abbey church was 'plucked down' by Edward Holcroft. He made a thorough job of it. The mansion he built out of the monastic parts passed in due course to the Cholmondeleys, Lords of Delamere. This in its turn fell into semi-ruin during the 3rd Lord Delamere's African adventures in the early twentieth century. Visitors to the empty hall in

▼ **Below**: *The Cathedral of St Asaph.*

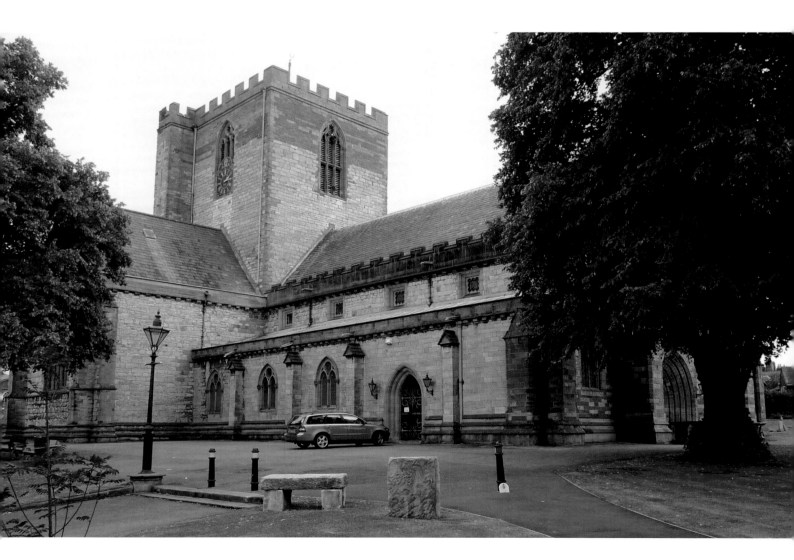

the 1970s may remember the sinister smell of decay that pervaded the place and the great fruiting bodies of dry rot that bulged out from the timberwork. Now it has been smartened up as the golf clubhouse, and a row of superior houses lines the driveway. The abbey precinct, which became the park of the country house, is now, as we have seen, a golf course. The church of Whitegate, which still stands just outside the abbey precinct, was the chapel maintained by the monastery for the locals – the capella ante portas. Remarkably, it retains its late medieval timber frame under an unpromising exterior of Victorian brick.

Chester Cathedral, once the Benedictine abbey of St Werburgh, is lost in an entirely different way. At the dissolution the abbey's future was in doubt, and a few elements such as the dormitory were lost. But in 1541 the king elevated it as a new cathedral, the centre of a vast but underendowed diocese encompassing Cheshire, Lancashire and part of Westmorland and Cumberland. Unlike Vale Royal, therefore, the church survived. Over the years it was maltreated in sundry ways – the north-west tower becoming the bishop's wine cellar, for example – but the real problem was the soft red sandstone of which it was constructed. By the mid-nineteenth century it was in a shocking state, the external carving almost eroded away, parapets and pinnacles gone, elegant traceries simplified. Along came George Gilbert Scott. His great restoration, just one of a series, was chronicled by his faithful clerk of works, James Frater, whose diary is preserved in the cathedral archive. The story is not so simple, of course, but essentially it was Scott who worked it over from end to end and top to bottom, giving it a new surface, a new silhouette and much conjectural detail. What we see on the outside today is largely not the medieval building but a nineteenth-century one. Scott was defensive about this: 'The external stonework of this cathedral was so horribly and lamentable decayed, as to reduce it to a mere wreck, like a mouldering sandstone cliff.'

If we return to St Asaph we find that the cathedral that was lost through war was, by the orders of Edward I, rebuilt on its old site. In 1578 there was another attempt to move the see to a more populous place when Robert Dudley, Earl of Leicester and an extreme Protestant, started to build a new cathedral in Denbigh. A plain box with equally plain round-arched windows, it would have been the first major church built for a Protestant ministry. But he never finished it.

In the nineteenth century Gilbert Scott was working on the restoration of St Asaph. 'This has not been an interesting work,' he said bluntly. The chancel is partly his, as are the floors and roofs and much of the furnishing. Much survives, however, of the 1382 rebuilding, distinguished by the double- or triple-sunk chamfer on columns and doorways without capitals that is so characteristic of Edward I's masons. It is a fine and dignified building, not showy or spectacular in any way but big-boned and handsomely proportioned. So St Asaph, in its modest way, has fared pretty well.

In November 1278 the king and queen were in Bury St Edmunds. Edmund, king and martyr, was especially venerated by royalty, as is proved by his portrayal in the exquisite Wilton Diptych of Richard II displayed today in the National Gallery, London. Perhaps Edward and Eleanor rode out to the place of his coronation, the lost – and found – place now called Chapel Barn (see chapter 3). A few days before Christmas they were at the shrine of St Alban, the first English martyr. The shrine was smashed by the reformers in 1539 but patiently pieced together again by the Victorians in 1872. It is amazing what can be recovered from apparent total loss, though nothing can restore its colour and gilding. Christmas at Windsor rounded off the year.

In sum, therefore, a church may be lost through war, like St Asaph or Coventry. It may be lost by complete or partial rebuilding, driven either by population growth (or shrinkage) or by changing taste, as Macclesfield. Like Vale Royal or Glastonbury, it may be lost through abolition; a vast treasury of our churches was lost in the dissolution of the monasteries in the 1530s and 1540s. Loss of a different kind may occur through sweeping restoration, as at Chester. John Ruskin certainly thought so, calling it 'the most total destruction which a building can suffer ... a destruction accompanied with a false description of the thing destroyed'. Indeed, the 'restoration' by Scott

of the Lady Chapel at Chester, started by R.C. Hussey in 1859, is now thought to be historically incorrect, for the restorers installed grouped lancets instead of the geometric tracery that was almost certainly there originally.

To these may be added a further factor, which is loss through failure. Failure to follow through, failure through waning enthusiasm, or simply empty coffers. Eleanor of Castile died in 1290, which probably stopped building operations in Macclesfield. Edward quarrelled with the monks of Vale Royal at much the same time, withdrawing all support to the abbey, which never therefore fulfilled the royal dream. Chester was always in a flux according to the fortunes of war, and the fabric of the cathedral church bears visible witness to this. Even at St Asaph the royal restitution may only have gone so far. In a later age, Dudley's new cathedral at Denbigh remains unfinished. The evidence suggests that, like the Episcopal cathedral in Oban (see chapter 7), all of these churches were partly lost in advance as it were, none of them being fully realised according to the original grand intention.

At the same time the churches at Chester, Macclesfield and especially St Asaph show how a church may survive against all the odds and even against all expectation. To reiterate, churches are long-lived structures, seldom disappearing completely but transforming themselves in response to changing circumstances. We may love to see a perfectly preserved church of another era, but a church which stands still while all around it changes is one that may not survive the next upheaval.

This Page: Vale Royal in Cheshire; the scant remains of the magnificent abbey founded by Edward I.

CHAPTER 1

A TOTAL LOSS

ST ALBAN CHEETWOOD, MANCHESTER

High and Low, the Church of England embraces a wide spectrum of belief and practice. St Alban Cheetwood, was the Highest of the High – its very dedication tells you that. Indeed, Bishop Prince Lee, a man of hot temper and strongly Protestant beliefs, refused to consecrate it because of its Romish ornaments and practices. Like many Anglo-Catholic outposts it was placed in one of the poorest districts of town, where the splendour of its ritual made the greatest contrast with the drab surroundings. Prayers were offered for the Pope as well as the Archbishop of Canterbury, and the Catholic Missal – in Latin – was preferred to the Book of Common Prayer. An Angelus bell, given in 1929 and rung daily, was inscribed 'Sancta Maria, Mater Dei, ora pro nobis peccatoribus'. A description of St Alban's Day in June 1939 gives a flavour: 'The church was packed and the uniformed organisations on parade. It was a wonderful sight with the crystal and jewelled crucifix gleaming through the incense and the rich banners giving colour and movement. The parish procession wound its way through the streets with a band and singing. Fr Glenday, grey-headed in cope and biretta, and followed by his dog Cracker, was at the centre of this happy homely occasion.' It was the Church of England's ordination of the first women as priests in 1994 that led to a mass defection and the closure of the church.

Cheetwood had once been a charming district of cottages, smallholdings and market gardens just outside and uphill from the city centre, but by the 1850s, when St Alban was built, it was a sea of brick pits and works dominated by the courthouse and monstrous prison which had taken the place of the ancient Strangeways Hall and its park.

The architect Joseph Stretch Crowther drew on his great knowledge of medieval Gothic in designing St Alban, especially that of the Decorated period. Beautifully turned arches, fine proportions and crisp carvings distinguished the interior, with the richest diapering and arcading reserved for the polygonal chancel. Money had run out, however, before the exterior could be completed to plan, leaving the intended soaring steeple as a stump and much of the carving unfinished. To make matters worse, it was badly damaged in the Blitz, when the roof was shaken and all the glass blown out. Nevertheless, standing high on a bluff above the rise of Waterloo Street, it was a notable landmark in an impoverished district.

After closure the church was made secure while options for its future were

St Alban Cheetwood, Manchester, January 1998. The south wall has already gone, the roof in tatters, allowing the winter sun to shine through.

discussed – at least that was the plan. The locals, however, had other ideas. Temporary fencing and boarding up rapidly proved utterly ineffectual. Stolen cars were raced and crashed around it, fires lit, glass and statuary smashed. Lead and slates rained down from the high roofs, their fall cushioned by abandoned mattresses so that some at least could be rescued and sold off. The diocese found itself faced with an emergency situation; something had to be done before somebody killed themselves.

And so a decision was taken: it would have to be demolished. The job was done in about seven weeks in all, during January–March 1998, in the dead of winter.

Demolishing a church is not easy. It is mostly air, surrounded by a thin envelope and structure of stone; no partitions, no intermediate floors or stairs. It is too tall to be easily scaffolded. Gothic architecture depends on balancing stresses and strains. Demolish one arch and all the rest are liable to fall on top of you, like a row of dominoes.

It was fascinating to watch as the demolition gang evolved their methods. They soon found out that carved stones were worth money, so the job had to be done with some delicacy. To anyone interested in buildings and building processes it was a revelation, akin to being able to watch a medieval church or cathedral being built but speeded up, and in reverse.

Crowther was always at pains to provide high-level access to his churches, as the medieval cathedral builders had been, so that churchwardens would have no excuse for not cleaning out the gutters. The narrow stair turrets flanking the chancel arch, their pointed tops punctuating the skyline, are a Crowther trademark. Even when half the building was gone, workmen would shimmy up one of the turrets to emerge, dizzy and breathless, on the very apex of the wall and start loosening the stones. The foreman used the bucket of a digger – not a medieval tool,

▶ **Right**: *St Alban. Now the nave roofs have gone, and so has the south arcade.*

this – at its highest reach to bring the stones down. Down below great fires were fed with the doors and roof timbers, providing somewhere to warm up and, incidentally, adding much to the drama of the scene.

The big surprise was that St Alban's, Cheetwood, never really beautiful in life, attained a couple of weeks of transcendent beauty before its final end. With few slates left, and no outer walls, the low winter sun shone straight through the building, picking out the elegant arcades, the delicate carving and sharply delineating the remaining tracery. Set off by the frosty ground and a couple of huge bonfires, the drama of the scene in such drab and nondescript surroundings was astounding. Tintern is no idle comparison. Crowther was a scholarly architect, the author of two giant volumes of measured drawings, *Churches of the Middle Ages*. A comparison of his church at Bury, which survives, with the nave of Tintern is by no means a fatuous exercise.

The last stages of the demolition threw up more instruction, and a final puzzle. How to take the tower down? After much head-scratching the foreman decided the only way to deal with it was to mound up its lower arches with earth and rubble, so that their carvings would be protected while he drove his digger up to the higher levels. It could then be taken down directly, stone by stone. We were now observing an even earlier method of building – in reverse – for is this not how the Egyptians built the pyramids?

Right at the end, when almost everything had gone, a muddy lump of stone appeared amongst the sludge and rubble. It showed a hint of a carved surface. When it had been recovered and the embedded pebbles and muck washed out, the carved decoration proved to be an exquisite length of Greek honeysuckle frieze. It was Ionic to be precise, and modelled accurately upon the frieze of the Erechtheion in Athens. This was a complete anomaly. What on earth was it doing under a Victorian Gothic church?

The best explanation I can come up with is that it had been used as hardcore in the foundations. History records that the men of the parish dragged stone and rubble for the foundations up the hill from Strangeways Hall, which was being demolished in

1858 for Alfred Waterhouse's new Assize Courts and gaol. Images of the vanished hall suggest that it may have had Greek detailing. Strangeways Hall has long gone, and so in the Blitz have the Assize Courts. It is strange to think of the slender thread of events that can determine whether a relic survives or is lost for ever.

What is left of St Alban's, Cheetwood? After the demolition, a shop on Cheetham Hill was set up as a chapel, opening as a new St Alban. Later this moved to Higher Broughton, but in communion with the orthodox rather than the Anglican church. Of the church itself, there is no sign. A total loss. New anywheresville housing crowds close, although the actual footprint of the building is left to waste ground and Japanese knotweed. More may await any future archaeologist.

The honeysuckle stone survives, off-site, as do a few other decorative pieces. An exploratory visit to the archive room at Manchester Cathedral threw up one final relic. The head verger reached under a table and produced a flat box, evidently heavy. Sit down before I open this, he says. And there, on a bed of deepest blue velvet, rested none other than the great silver processional crucifix with its crystal and jewels that had once gleamed through the incense of St Alban's, Cheetwood.

▼ **Below**: *Gone. The site is cleared, the machines finally at rest. Manchester city centre is in the background, with the 'minaret' of Strangeways gaol.*

▶ **Right**: *St Alban. On a dark winter's evening, just the tower and the apse remain.*

CHAPTER 2

ABOLISHED

~

Britain is full of melancholy monastic ruins, widespread testimony to the piety of the Middle Ages and the rapaciousness of Henry VIII. From the greatest, such as Fountains, Tintern or Melrose, to the least, such as Birkenhead Priory on its lonely headland, or the island house at Iona, monastic buildings follow the same logical pattern. The church is cross-shaped and oriented east–west. Sheltering in the angle between nave and transept is the square cloister, the centre of monastic life, and round this are ranged, in a set order, the domestic offices – chapterhouse, dormitory, refectory and so on. This means that even when a monastery has almost completely disappeared, such as Dieu la Cres in Staffordshire, given a few clues, it is easy to work out where the various components must be.

There were once, it is estimated, as many as 650 monastic foundations in England. Between them they owned and cultivated maybe a quarter of the land. The number in Wales was around sixty, including such well-known sites as Tintern and Valle Crucis, and eighty-four major foundations in Scotland, although these numbers may be arrived at by different methods and not be strictly comparable.

The monasteries were centres of piety and learning, dispensing charity, medicine and education. At the forefront of an agricultural revolution they were also, perhaps surprisingly, pioneers of industrial methods such as iron ore extraction and smelting. By the sixteenth century they had grown fat and sometimes lax, and were seen by some as ripe for the picking.

For the monasteries of England and Wales the end was sudden. In just ten years, between 1530 and 1540, the whole lot were swept away. The first blow came from within the Church, when Cardinal Wolsey obtained leave from the Pope to dissolve the smaller houses in order to endow colleges in Oxford and Ipswich. The rest tumbled with astonished speed. In 1535–6 Henry VIII dissolved all the foundations in England and Wales of below £200 income per annum. A revolt in the north, the Pilgrimage of Grace of 1536, was suppressed with great savagery and mass executions in 1537. This was followed by a final Act in 1539 which confiscated all the property of the remaining great houses, leaving their communities to surrender with greater or lesser grace. The last to go, in 1540, was King Harold's foundation at Waltham Abbey. The only foundation never to surrender, even though cast adrift, was Syon.

Rather than being killed off, the monasteries of Scotland died, and it was a gradual rather than a sudden death. By the 1550s they were usually ruled by secular commendators who were only interested in the revenues, and no new recruits were

taken in. Some carried on after a fashion into the seventeenth century. In the end, however, the Scottish reformation, initiated in 1560, was more complete, because cathedrals and bishops were abolished as well.

John Leland was a contemporary witness, in some instances our only one. In 1533 he had been authorised by Henry VIII to examine the libraries of the monastic houses up and down the land. His unique access gave us a description of them on the eve of their dissolution, though he cannot have been fully aware that this was to be their fate. Despite his report, the libraries, the most important intellectual capital of the country, were largely dispersed and lost a few years later. After the dissolution he undertook six extended journeys, or Itineraries, between 1538 and 1543. The first one was through Wales, and his itinerary of 1542 took him to the West Country, but otherwise we are not certain where he went or when.

GLASTONBURY

'There is no religious foundation in England whose history carries us so far back as that of Glastonbury. Its origins really are lost in the mists of antiquity.' So wrote M.R. James, scholar, antiquary and writer of ghost stories, in *Abbeys*, published in 1925 by the Great Western Railway.

By the time of the Norman Conquest, Glastonbury was already the richest and most venerable in the land. Comparable with Cluny in Burgundy, at the Reformation it was second in fame and wealth only to Westminster. It was commonly said that if the Abbess of Shaftesbury could only marry the Abbot of Glastonbury they would hold more land and have greater wealth than the King of England.

This is a place where it is hard to separate the concrete evidence from the fabulous, indeed perhaps it is not necessary to do so. Did Joseph of Arimathea really come here? Did his staff really grow into the holy thorn which flowers at Christmastide? Are King Arthur and Queen Guinevere really buried in the choir?

What seems certain is that sometime in the second or third centuries AD Christian missionaries built a little church of wattles on the island called Avalon. Marshes surrounded the site, but the improbably dramatic Tor rose close by. In the seventh century a protective shell of timber and lead was built over the little chapel. Immediately to the east and in line with it a stone church was built, which grew in stages over the years. After a calamitous fire swept through the site in 1184, the old chapel was immediately rebuilt in ornate Norman style, and the rest followed bit by bit. Eventually the whole ensemble, like a great ship of faith, was even longer than old St Paul's.

Glastonbury with its great wealth was vastly tempting to Henry VIII, but his inquisitors found very little evidence of wrongdoing in the abbey's affairs to justify abolishing it. The abbey was still building and still recruiting novices to the religious life. Nevertheless in 1539 Glastonbury Abbey and all it stood for was dissolved, bringing to an end twelve centuries of religious and cultural life. Abbot Whiting,

the mildest of rebels, and two of his monks were put to death with the utmost brutality on Glastonbury Tor, fulfilling an ancient prophesy:

> *When a whiteing on ye Torr is caught:*
> *Then shall ye Abbey comme to nawght.*

'Of these immense buildings, very little now remains; and what still exists exhibits woeful marks of the effects of time. In the great church the havoc made is truly deplorable. That mighty fabric, the erecting of which must have exhausted a quarry, is now only a heap of ruins.' This was the description in *The Beauties of England and Wales*, 1813. Today the heap of ruins has been cleared away, tidied up, weeded, labelled, and is presented thus to the idle visitor.

The only part of the church which retains

much integrity is the western Lady Chapel that was built in a hurry after the fire of 1184 to replace the wattle church. Carefully photographed, we can get a good impression of its original beauty, although we still have to imagine the floor, which has collapsed into the crypt chapel, the roof, the glass and the colour. Otherwise only the Abbot's Kitchen stands pretty well complete. Its superb architecture gives an idea of the quality and ambition of the whole. The kitchen owes its survival to its fireproof construction. It served for a while as a Quaker meeting house (up to 1690), and then as a depot for the sale of pillaged stone. The nearby Abbey Barn, too, beautifully proportioned with the four evangelists carved on its four gables, gives us an inkling of how much was lost. Analogy may tell us more. The fine church of St Stephen in Bristol, with its spectacular tower, was a dependant of Glastonbury. The architect of the fifteenth-century work there is known, one Benet Crosse; there is even a drawing of the porch by him. By a long shot, maybe he worked at Glastonbury, too. Nearer at hand, the tower of Glastonbury's parish church and the fine hostelry of the George and Pilgrim were both built by John Selwood, abbot 1456–93.

Glastonbury Abbey has since 1907 been owned by the Church of England, and is the focus of a big Christian pilgrimage in June. For the rest of the year, however, it is run as though it was simply another ancient monument, taking no part in the life of the place. While Glastonbury town and environs might be seething with undirected spiritual energy, reaching a peak on the winter or summer solstice, the abbey is dead. Like Hagia Sofia in Istanbul, or St Sophia in Kiev, it has been turned from a great

◀ **Opposite page**: *Glastonbury. The chapel of St Joseph at the west end, rebuilt in 1184–9.*

◀ **Left**: *The only intact building at Glastonbury is the Abbot's Kitchen.*

Glastonbury. The north door of St Joseph's Chapel is depicted in romantic decay.

centre of religious power into a museum. The ruins are open to the public in the customary British manner: all shaven lawns and admonitory notices, standard opening hours, ticket office, shop and toilets. Discounts for students and pensioners. The visitor centre interprets the place in the past tense, or worse, in the dreaded conditional 'would have been', hoping to stimulate mild interest in the amateur archaeologist, but anticipating disappointment in those expecting a magnificent and poetic ruin like Tintern or Fountains. The banal presentation deprives the place of much of its power.

In truth there is not a great deal to see, but much to engage the imagination. Glastonbury, in spite of all, has an extra numinous dimension in comparison with most monastic sites, and its mysterious properties can be infectious. The first custodian appointed by the Church of England, Frederick Bligh Bond (1864–1935), became something of a mystic, claiming that he had been guided in his excavations by voices from the past. He believed that the dimensions of the abbey had been determined by the occult science of gematria, where numerical values are assigned to letters and phrases. That way madness lies, but he could be right. It is recorded that there were geometric markings on the floor of the church. Bligh Bond's psychical research was strongly disapproved of by the Church, and in 1921 he was sacked.

The immense length of the lost abbey church from the east end.

COCKERSAND ABBEY

'Standeth verï blekely and object to all wynddes'
(John Leland, c. 1537)
'All the human being can think of is shelter; and there is none'
(Brian Marshall, 2001)

Glastonbury in its fertile vale was always famous, its monastery renowned. The modest Premonstratensian abbey of Cockersand was at the other end of the scale. It stood on the extreme edge of the Irish Sea in north Lancashire, overlooking the Lune estuary and vast tidal sands. There is nothing to break the nag of the wind which blows almost constantly. But on a rare day of stillness and sunshine it is a lovely spot. Lapwings dot the fields or carry out aerial displays. Flights of swans pass overhead, their feathers whistling, to graze on the fields inland. Eider ducks utter low comments out on the mud flats. Yellowhammers sing in the windblown hedgerows. It is a place of wide views in an immense flat landscape. Pilling and Fleetwood lie across the water, with Blackpool Tower behind. Across the flat fields the black silhouette of Lancaster can be seen against a Pennine backdrop, and beyond that the Ashton Memorial and the university with its drooping wind turbine. Heysham nuclear power station looms. The Cumbrian coast and fells stretch into the far distance. On a clear day the sharp-eyed may see Piel Castle, right at the tip of the Cumbrian peninsula.

The abbey stands where a religious recluse called Hugh Garth, held in great reverence locally, built a little oratory where the sands met the shore. It was the landing place for the hazardous cross-sands routes that saved a long trek inland around the estuaries. The abbey provided a light and hospitality for travellers. There is still a little lighthouse out on the sands.

The Premonstratensians were a strict order, often choosing a challenging environment in which to settle, as did their brothers at Shap in Westmorland. The neighbouring Conishead and Cartmel Priories in Lakeland Lancashire were, in contrast, Augustinians, and not so strict. It is worth remembering the European dimension of these monastic orders, which knew no national boundaries. Averbode, near Diest in Belgium, is Premonstratensian and still thriving, having seventy-eight canons in 2011. Another is Strahov in Prague with its famous libraries.

There is not much to be seen at Cockersand today, but the little that there is has considerable power. As the byroad winds its right-angled way across the flat fields to the coast a slight but significant rise can be seen. These 8 or 9 feet above the general level were enough to provide a solid site for the abbey to be built. Church, cloister, dormitory and so on are represented by mere scatterings of stones and a couple of inarticulate lumps but, all alone, the polygonal chapterhouse stands complete. A very odd sight it is, too, for it is half buried in the sand and turf, and its windows are walled up. Apart from the chapterhouse the scanty ruins tell you very little. According to the excavation, the church was unusually narrow at only 20 feet wide, or seven paces, but the findings of the Swarbrick excavation were

not at all definite about the width or lack of aisles. In any case, Premonstratensian planning was frequently unmethodical, so you can't necessarily guess.

On a rare occasion the chapterhouse door might be open. Then you can fall out of the wind and rain into a lit and warm enclosure, to find quite a few people sheltering and steaming gently. The space is a revelation. A central column with clustered shafts and foliage cap rises to a beautiful vault arching over to the eight corners. More shafting and arches articulate the blocked windows, but the peripheral stone bench and column bases are all buried, for Cockersand chapterhouse owes its survival to its use as a mausoleum for the Dalton family and the burials have raised the floor level.

The Great Inventory of 1536 survives, and can tell us a good deal more. The church had a steeple and six bells – four 'in accord', i.e. in tune, 'two out of accord', so we can imagine what they sounded like. There were nine windows in the chancel, so that makes one at the east end and four each side. Eleven windows in the nave, making it five each side. Ten bays in all if we add in the crossing. There were five chapels plus a detached lady chapel. The thirty choir stalls were valued at £3.6s.8d., i.e. just over two shillings each. It has long been held that the stalls in Lancaster Priory come from Cockersand. If that is correct it gives an entirely different picture from the bleak image captured so far, for this is the most sumptuous woodwork imaginable, luxuriant with carved foliage and sinuous tracery. The rooms round the cloister are listed with their contents, including the great chest now at Thurnham Hall. The cloister was paved with patterned tiles, a few of which are shown in Lancaster Museum, along with some fragments of stained glass and their lead mountings.

The abbey was surrendered in 1539 by Abbot Poulton and twenty-two named canons. In 1537 there were, as well as the abbot and canons, fifty-seven servants and five poor men maintained by charity – perhaps nearly a hundred in all. The wage bill in 1536 was £46.16s.8d. Today there is nobody apart from a few walkers and birdwatchers, and some distant caravans.

▲ **Above**: *Cockersand Abbey. The lonely ruins on the Lancashire coast.*

◀ **Left**: *The interior of the chapter house, preserved as a family mausoleum.*

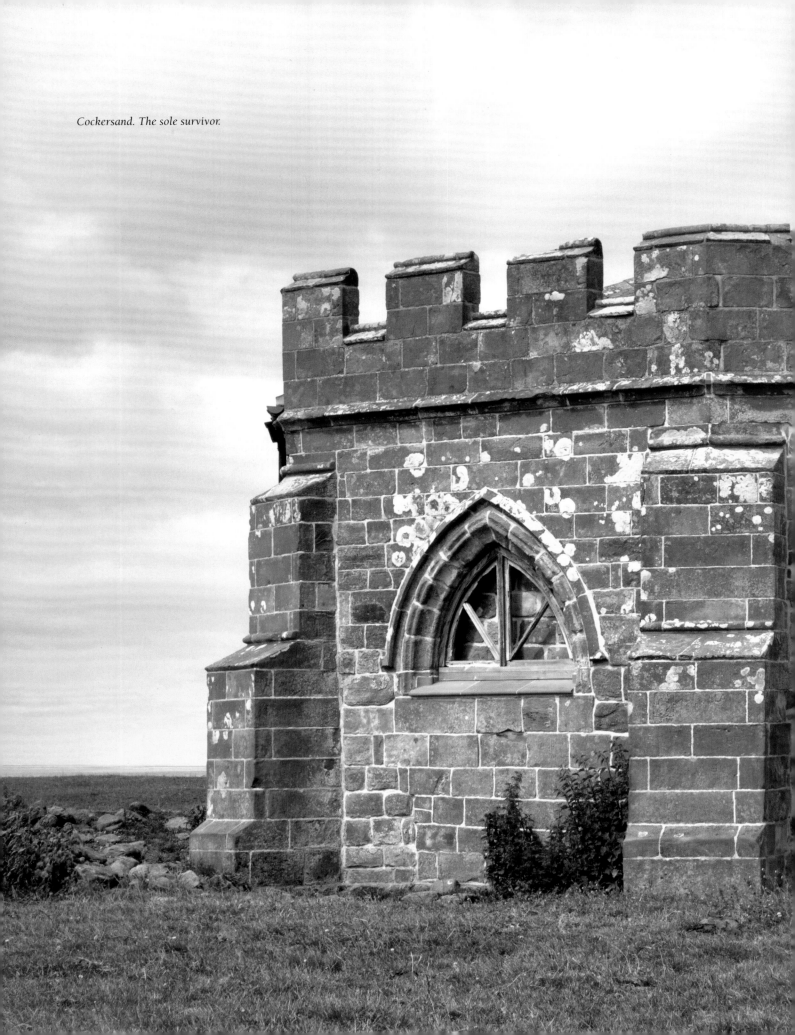

Cockersand. The sole survivor.

CALDER ABBEY AND SEATON NUNNERY

Calder Abbey is not so much lost as hidden away and forgotten. It lies a mile or two inland from the unfrequented west coast of Cumbria, between Whitehaven and Ravenglass. The familiar monastic sites are in the care of English Heritage, CADW, Historic Scotland, and are maintained to the same standard brief. Ruined walls are kept in good repair, which is an odd way to spend money if you think about it. Parts may be scaffolded while work goes on to prevent further ruination. They are kept clear of vegetation and surrounded by well-mown grass. The site is fenced off and guarded by a ticket office and shop. It is rare to see a monastic site as Wordsworth, Turner and Cotman saw them, romantically decaying,

luxuriant with creepers and nesting birds. Calder is such a place. Here is an ideally picturesque abbey ruin, hushed and forgotten, half drowned in long grass and nettles, its stones overgrown, the abode of nesting birds and burrowing animals. No ticket office, no shaven lawns, no helpful metal signs, no interpretation boards or audio guides. It is just there, crumbling gently.

Calder was never rich. Its very foundation story is unfortunate. In 1135 a party of twelve monks and their elected abbot set out from Furness Abbey at the southern tip of the Cumbrian peninsula intent on founding a daughter house. They settled here and no doubt started to build, but within four years had been driven out by marauding Scots. Returning in despair to Furness, they were turned away at the gate

– presumably because an abbey cannot have two abbots. On they wandered in the wilderness, eventually fetching up at Byland in north Yorkshire. Here at last the community found a home. As time went by Furness and Byland grew into great and wealthy abbeys, but what of Calder?

A second colony set out from Furness in 1143. By now William FitzDuncan, the leader of the marauding Scots, was by right of marriage Lord Egremont, and so the second colony was permitted to take root at Calder.

The modest abbey that was built over the next half-century survives quite well. The west front stands to the level of the windowsill, and the north arcade is complete with its elegant but fairly low arches. In contrast the four crossing arches reach tall and wide, supporting a low tower which may perhaps have been defensive. Under the crossing lie three knights in chain mail, with triangular shields. The dormitory reaches out to the south on an upper floor, as was usual over a range of storehouses.

Calder was always vulnerable. More raids are recorded in 1216 and 1332, and the nave of the abbey church shows signs of downsizing which may be related to this. At the dissolution in 1536 it was valued at just £50, and there were nine monks in residence.

A Georgian house was built upon the south side of the cloister, although the word Georgian hardly conjures up the gaunt house with its patched-up plaster we see today. In 1906 a new owner, the Manchester solicitor Thomas

◀ **Opposite page**: *Calder Abbey. Romantically overgrown ruin of the dormitory range.*

▲ **Above**: *Calder. The abbey church, still romantically overgrown.*

Harrison Rymer, commissioned an opulent extension from the Arts and Crafts architect George Faulkner Armitage. Today this house is simply sleeping, as is the whole site.

Why the neglect, the sleeping beauty? Climb the low hill to Ponsonby church for the answer, for and there, spread out at your feet, is the vast nuclear facility once called Calder Hall, then Winscale, and now Sellafield.

Not every monastic settlement attained great wealth and power, nor for that matter was it always a great blessing. Some houses remained in obscurity and poverty, nevertheless managing to keep going for three hundred years.

The nunnery of Seaton was founded a few miles south of Calder in around 1190 or 1200, probably by Henry Fitzarthur. It stood not far from the village of Bootle in west Cumberland, close to the sea but prudently out of sight of maritime marauders. The priory's finances were so poor, its troubles so

great, that the foundation charter was lost and the nuns had to forge another one. When it was dissolved in 1536 there were just two nuns and a novice in residence. Its value was put at £13.17s.4d. Yet what we find on the site today shows that the community was not negligible, nor was life there devoid of beauty.

Like the little nunnery on the island of Iona, Seaton has an atmosphere of great peace. The monasteries, however modest, got their pick of the best spots. There is not much to see, and it is not consciously preserved, but still standing in the small garden between Seaton Hall and its farmyard is the east gable of the priory church. Three tall lancets of equal height, lightly decorated with wallflowers and toadflax, are elegantly shafted in the Early English style. From the fragment of south wall that remains, it seems that the shafting carried on round the east end of the church, leaving a walkway behind. The effect (and possible origin) of this can be seen in the east end of St Bees church, another monastic foundation, further up the coast. The farmhouse, Seaton Hall, looks largely Victorian but its position exactly reflects that of the nuns' refectory and dormitory. The small square of ground between church and house shows the diminutive size of their cloister.

◄ **Opposite top**: *Calder. The west end of the church and a glimpse of the house.*

◄ **Opposite bottom**: *The humble Nunnery of Seaton in Cumbria. The farmhouse incorporates the refectory and dormitory.*

▼ **Below**: *Three tall lancets are all that is left of the nuns' church.*

SYON

Syon House, the London seat of the Dukes of Northumberland, occupies an enviable Thames-side spot opposite Kew Gardens. A plain foursquare mansion hiding great splendour within, it stands among the last remaining Thames-side water meadows. It is a pretty spot but, like Kew, oppressed by incessant noise from the Heathrow flight path.

The name comes from the great Brigittine nunnery that once stood here, but few great churches are lost quite as thoroughly as Syon. This was one of the greatest and richest abbeys in the land,

founded and patronised by royalty. In 1539 there were still 52 choir nuns, 4 lay sisters, 12 brothers and 5 lay brothers in residence, and yet today there is apparently nothing left.

Syon was different from any other British abbey, and followed a different plan. Founded by King Henry V on the Middlesex bank of the Thames between Isleworth and Twickenham in 1415, the year of Agincourt, it was an outpost of the Scandinavian order of St Birgitta, or Bridget: the Brigittines. Her rule stipulated a community of up to 60 enclosed nuns under a governing abbess, with a male complement of 13 priests, 4 deacons and 8 lay brethren. Segregation

of the sexes was strict; each had their own cloister, one on each side of the great church, and the church itself had to be wide enough for the two sides to be divided with an iron screen.

The quadrangular plan of the house, which is aligned exactly with the compass, invites the supposition that it was built out of the abbey cloister. In that case the lost church would have wrapped around its north and east sides. This would be an entirely reasonable guess anywhere else, and is indeed the case at Vale Royal, Newstead and Stoneleigh. But not here.

As far as we can tell, Syon abbey church was unlike anything else in England. It was huge. A recent reconstruction suggests something like an enormous aisled barn, its width the entire width of the house we see today. The 136 feet of the long gallery indicates this. Its length was more than twice that. The present Syon House, in other words, sits on just part of the Brigittines' great

▼ **Below**: *Syon. The great house stands on the site of the Brigittine church.*

church. The two cloisters, one for men and one for women, were ranged to its north and south.

To visualise it by analogy we need to call up the substantial remains of its sister church near Tallinn in Estonia, a place called Pirita. Even in ruin this is one of the most impressive structures in that country, with its enormous west gable reaching up 100 feet, its massive buttresses testifying to the vanished vaulting, and its vast emptiness within. It was a hall church, with aisles the same height as the nave.

Excavations at Pirita have uncovered hundreds of domestic items: decorated pots, knives, buckles, book clasps, candle-holders, games and a fascinating mason's plan of a net vault scratched on the clay of a brick.

Scattered far and wide are the few remnants of Syon's famous library, or libraries. There were at least two, one for the brothers and one for the nuns. All carry or carried the distinctive Syon mark and classification, and some are inscribed with the names of individual owners: Susan Purefeye, Elizabeth Monton, Clemence Tresham. One book in particular seems to tell a tale of suppressed love. The Incendium Amoris of Rolle belonged to Joanna Sewell 'reclusa'. Intertwined initials JS and JR and exclamations in the marginalia of a book suggest an incipient and absolutely illicit love affair between Sister Joanna Sewell and James Greenhalgh, a Carthusian monk of Sheen across the river, who may have given her the book. Brayley's comment (London and Middlesex, 1816, Vol. IV, p. 362) comes to mind: 'It would, perhaps, be hard to devise an institution more ingeniously calculated to torture the human passions into habits of immorality, than that designed by the erring zeal of St. Bridget.' They were discovered, and Greenhalgh was sent away to Coventry and then Hull. Joanna Sewell remained at Syon, where she died in 1532 and was buried '*iuxta gerras*' – beside the screen in the church.

The most dazzling survival is the Syon cope, now displayed at the Victoria & Albert Museum. This fabulous object with its multitude of embroidered angels was made in about 1320, so it is actually a century older than Syon, and must have been given

▶ **Right**: *The Syon cope, now in the V & A, recalls something of the splendour of the lost abbey.*

to the abbey, perhaps at its founding. The tortuous tale of its survival sums up the subsequent history of the community.

The abbey was well run and there was never any convincing evidence of the wrongdoing that afflicted many of the monasteries. Nevertheless, Henry VIII and his commissioners were anxious to seize such a rich prize. In 1534 the most distinguished of the brethren, Richard Reynolds, refused to acknowledge Henry as head of the Church. He was thrown into the Tower and, on 4 May 1535, hanged at Tyburn. 'A sharp breakfast', he is said to have commented as his fellow accused were disembowelled, 'but we dine in heaven.' The religious of Syon, alone among the monasteries, never did surrender. Instead, in 1539, they were turned out, taking the keys and abbey seal with them.

The nuns scattered in groups, each maintaining a semblance of community life. In 1541–2 the deserted abbey, now crown property, held Henry VIII's repudiated queen Catherine Howard while her fate was decided. She went to the block. Henry's own coffin rested here in 1547 on its way for burial at Windsor. It is recorded that during the night the coffin burst, and dogs were found licking up the effluvia: just deserts, maybe.

In 1557 Queen Mary, hoping to turn back the Protestant tide, summoned the scattered nuns back from the Low Countries to a revived abbey; but their stay was brief. In 1559 Elizabeth and her parliament threw them out again. They fled back to Flanders, and after years of hardship and wandering ended up in Lisbon. When the 2nd Duke of Northumberland,

now in possession, met the abbess there, she remarked that she still had the keys to Syon. 'Indeed Madam?' replied the Duke politely, 'but I have altered the locks.' All this time, recruiting new postulants from England, they must have had the precious cope with them, along with a few books. In 1861 they were finally able to return, settling in 1887 in Devon. But sadly in 2013 this, the only religious community to have survived intact from before the Reformation, finally succumbed to old age and the lack of new vocations. Adversity can give more strength than comfort, the long journey more rewarding than the arrival. At Pirita, however, a new Brigittine convent, built alongside the shell of the old, was completed and consecrated in 2001.

CHAPTER 3

LOST AND FOUND

~

THE ROYAL CHAPEL OF ST STEPHEN, WESTMINSTER

In the afternoon of Thursday, 16 October 1834, a small party of visitors was shown around the House of Lords by the resident housekeeper, Mrs Wright. Parliament was in recess, so all was quiet. The Lords at that time sat in the White Chamber of the ancient palace of Whitehall, having moved there in 1801 from the Queen's Chamber.

The visitors were worried by the smell of burning which seemed to pervade the place, the slight miasma of smoke and the warmth of the stone floor which they could feel even through their boots. Mrs Wright reassured them, however, that all was in order, knowing that a couple of workmen were engaged at the furnace below in burning thousands of old tally sticks, a simple means of accounting debt and repayment, that had accumulated over the centuries. At any rate, nothing was done. Only at 6.30 that evening was the alarm raised, and by then it was far too late. The flues from the furnace had overheated, the floors had been smouldering for hours. Eventually wood burst into flame, flame spread rapidly through the warren of buildings and the biggest fire since the Great Fire of London raged all night. Thousands flocked to witness the spectacle, thronging the bridges and the far shore and crowding on to boats on the river below. Among them were Charles Dickens and J.M.W. Turner. The champion of Gothic, A.W.N. Pugin, recorded gleefully how 'the old walls [of Westminster Hall] stood triumphantly in the midst of ruin, while brick walls and framed sashes etc. fell faster than a pack of cards'. His future collaborator, the architect Charles Barry, had leapt off the Brighton coach on seeing the flames, and began to make plans for a new palace as soon as he got home.

By morning almost the whole of the ancient palace had been consumed, save only Westminster Hall and a few other fragments. While the stones were still hot, indeed while parts of the palace were still burning, the artist George Scharf was clambering over the ruins recording as much as he could of the ancient buildings before they were cleared away.

While the Lords sat in the White Chamber, the Commons were still occupying the former Royal Chapel of St Stephen which had been given to them after its dissolution in 1547. Over the three centuries they had striven to make it more comfortable and better ventilated, while squeezing in extra MPs from Scotland and Ireland, until it had long since lost any appearance of a chapel. By 1834 almost nothing of it was visible; indeed, its very existence had almost been

forgotten. Only by crawling underneath the members' seats could an energetic antiquary such as John Carter or Richard Smirke gain a glimpse of the exquisite painted decoration of the original walls. Above the false ceiling an unofficial visitors' gallery had been contrived, from which the doings of parliament could be glimpsed below through the hole above the great chandelier. Here in the gloom could be seen the tops of the great medieval windows and fragments of their rich tracery. Otherwise there was hardly a hint of the building's origin, save the odd parliamentary customs, which continue to this day, of sitting in two adversarial sets of 'choir stalls' facing each other (anyone who has sung in a cathedral choir will immediately recognise this as 'Dec' and 'Can'), bowing to the Speaker, who sat where the altar had been, and voting Aye or No by passing through one or other of the two doors of the screen.

Now everything had been burnt away: wainscot, benches, gallery, chandelier, ceiling, all reduced to ash. Briefly, the bones of the Royal Chapel of St Stephen miraculously reappeared. There were the great windows of the upper chapel with their elaborately carved spandrels, and the deep buttresses between, with their weighty pinnacles, and the twin turrets that faced the river. Inside the walls was the delicate medieval screen, which had not been visible for centuries. Scharf was up there for three weeks, making a series of rapid sketches with which he intended to make a panorama. But then the tottering shell was demolished

▲ **Above**: *The Royal Chapel of St Stephen and its cloister, briefly revealed after the great fire of 1834, was painted by George Scharf while it was still smouldering.*

and lost for ever, leaving only the undercroft – whose vault had saved it from the fire – and part of the adjacent cloister.

Incidentally, George Scharf's Westminster panorama has its own tale of Lost and Found. It went missing, presumed lost, in about 1860. In 1991 a section of it was spotted in an antique shop in South Africa. The buyer notified one of the Westminster MPs, and it was eventually bought back to England. Somewhere is lurking its companion piece, the other half of his intended panorama.

The origins of the chapel go back to the thirteenth century. On 26 April 1248 King Henry III of England was in Paris for the ceremonial consecration of his cousin Louis IX's architectural jewel, La Sainte Chapelle. This had been built as a worthy setting for the most holy of holy relics, the Crown of Thorns, which Louis had purchased at fabulous cost. At Louis' invitation Henry was permitted to carry one

of the lesser relics in procession to the altar. La Sainte Chapelle was, and is, a building of fragile beauty, like a huge but delicate casket: a tall cage of stone and glass miraculously supporting a stone vault, somehow standing without the usual external paraphernalia of flying buttresses. Here was the ultimate symbol of sacred kingship. Henry, it was said, would have liked to carry the whole thing off in a horse and cart.

Instead, it was left to his son Edward I to found the Royal Chapel of St Stephen at Westminster. Standing at right angles to Westminster Hall, it was designed like La Sainte Chapelle on two floors. The undercroft chapel, low and vaulted, was for Palace servants and officials. The upper chapel, soaring high with enormous windows, was accessible only to members of the court and, of course, the king himself.

The chapel took many years to build. The undercroft, dedicated to St Mary, was completed in 1297, the upper chapel of St Stephen only in 1348, and the decoration continued until 1363. A small fan-vaulted cloister, built on two storeys like that of old St Paul's, stood in the angle between the chapel and Westminster Hall.

Ninety feet long, 28 wide and nearly 100 feet high, the chapel was built of stone from France and Oxfordshire. Dark marble was brought from Purbeck, timber from the royal forests, glass from Wells, iron from Spain. The whole of the interior was exquisitely painted and lavishly gilded, and the twelve huge windows were entirely filled with stained glass. Beneath each window was a row of eight painted figures, and sculpted figures stood in niches between each window. Gilded stars powdered the heavenly blue of the high roof.

While the calcined stones of the upper chapel had to be pulled down, the undercroft chapel of St Mary survived, although much damaged. Over the years since the Reformation it had served as a coal store, wine cellar and eventually as the Speaker's dining room. Restored and refurnished in Victorian style, it is a chapel once more, where members can be married or have their children baptised. The body of Margaret Thatcher lay in state here on 17 April 2013 before her funeral the following day. The upper chapel has been rebuilt by Barry and Pugin as St Stephen's Hall, a ceremonial corridor linking Westminster Hall with the Central Lobby of the Palace. The small cloister survives, too, though much repaired. As for the lost, found and then lost again chapel of St Stephen, it lives on in architectural history, often cited as one of the most influential of all English churches. It saw the first lierne vault of the late Decorated style in the lower chapel, while the upper vies with Gloucester as the pioneer of the English Perpendicular style.

◀ **Opposite page**: *St Stephen. An antiquarian record of the wall painting gives an idea of the overpowering richness of the chapel's original decoration.*

▼ **Below**: *The surviving vault of the undercroft chapel under repair.*

BRADFORD ON AVON

One day in 1857 the vicar of Bradford on Avon, Canon William Henry Rich Jones, a man of antiquarian interests, was looking out over his home town from the high vantage point of St Mary Tory. A gathering of the Wiltshire Archaeological Society was due to meet at Bradford, and the canon was mentally preparing a paper on the history of the parish. Naturally he intended to mention the recorded foundation in about the year 700 by St Aldhelm of a small monastic church, an 'ecclesiola', down by the River Avon. Its approximate position was known by the discovery of a burial site, but it was assumed that any trace of the building itself, in all probability a simple and perishable shelter, had long since gone.

Even now the stubborn label the Dark Ages clings to the centuries between the departure of the Romans and the coming of the Normans. When evidence is lacking it is all too easy to imagine life at that time to be short and brutal, and the dwellings and churches as crude and primitive, built of 'wattle and daub' or some such transitory materials.

However, on that day in 1857, amongst the jumble of roofs, steps and alleys in the town below him, Canon Jones noticed an intriguing conjunction and orientation of roofs in the place where St Aldhelm's chapel was known to have stood: a high roof and a lower one, both running east–west, and two roofs lower still and at right angles, making a cross shape. On making his way to the spot, however, there was nothing to be seen, so tight was the huddle of buildings and walls, so dense the growth of ivy.

However, in 1855 a chimney flue in the schoolroom, which stood by the river adjacent to the parish church, needed to be enlarged. Knocking out

Lost for centuries. The Saxon Chapel of St Lawrence at Bradford on Avon.

*The north side with its porticus
and applied decoration.*

part of the partition wall between the schoolroom and the schoolteacher's cottage in order to put in the stack, the workmen were surprised to discover, high up under the plaster, a flying angel. Sculpted in relief in stone, it seemed a most unlikely find. Further investigation revealed a second angel, its mirror image, on the other side. The two were taken down and mounted over the schoolroom door as a curiosity.

Now Canon Jones considered the two angels more carefully, comparing them with figures in early psalters and manuscripts. Could they have been part of a rood – a figure of the crucified Christ flanked by angels? And could they even date back to Aldhelm's time?

The next bit of the jigsaw fell into place in 1871 when Canon Jones read a newly issued text of William of Malmesbury's *Gesta Pontificum*, written in about 1120. In it William refers to Aldhelm's church at Bradford on Avon in the present tense, as though it still stood in his day, four centuries after its foundation. If then, why not now? Piece by piece, the building he had spotted from the hilltop was disinterred from the buildings round about and the different ownerships and uses to which its parts had been put. The chancel, for so it proved to be, had become a two-storey cottage, its chimney blocking up the chancel arch. This was purchased in 1872. New premises were found for the school, and then the offending flue could be removed, the chancel arch rebuilt and the two angels reinstated high above. Now the nave was revealed. Intermediate floors were removed, the two side doors were repaired, the north porticus cleared and restored. Unfortunately the south porticus, which had become the teacher's house, was eventually demolished except for two chunks of masonry left as sloping buttresses. Apart from that Aldhelm's little church stands fully revealed once more – and a very surprising thing it is, too.

Here is a sophisticated building, well constructed out of good ashlar stone. There is nothing crude or primitive about it, although its proportions are excessively tall and narrow to our eyes. The high walls are unexpectedly thin, not massive and thick as those of a Norman building would be. Its proportions, although odd, are of classical resonance, harking back to antiquity; perhaps that is why they look odd. The nave in elevation is a perfect square of ten paces. The chancel is as long as the nave is wide, and the north porticus or transept is as long as the chancel is wide. So all the parts of the building are mathematically related. Pilasters and arcading have been applied on the outside, perhaps at a later date, emphasising the classical proportions. The two doorways, likewise very tall and narrow, are exactly opposite one another, their jambs sloping inwards in a characteristic fashion. The few windows, set high, are well splayed to let in the maximum light.

Scholars will continue to argue about exactly how much of this building dates back to Aldhelm's foundation, but the little church of St Lawrence in Bradford on Avon, lost for centuries and found again in the 1870s, is one of the most complete and satisfying Anglo-Saxon churches remaining to us.

▶ **Right**: *Bradford on Avon. A glimpse through the Saxon Chapel, with its characteristically tall and narrow doorways.*

EYNHALLOW, ORKNEY

On 27 June 2007 the beautiful little two-master *Lily*, an Orkney yawl, landed on the island of Rousay, and the two mariners who built and sailed her put up at our hostel. The next day we were offered a sail to the 'holy island' of Eynhallow – that is a literal translation from Old Norse. However, a crossing like this can easily be frustrated. There the island lies, just across the water from Midhowe broch on Rousay, or from Gurness broch on the Orkney mainland. Yet it is also obvious even from the shore that the navigation of Eynhallow Sound is not to be undertaken lightly. Conflicting and vicious currents raise angry waves on the surface; the changing colour of the water marks out no-go areas. Reefs and rocks make the trip doubly hazardous.

Eynhallow, like so many of the small islands around our shores, was inhabited for centuries. The 1841 census recorded twenty-six people living here, belonging to four families. In the 1851 census there are none. The islanders had been struck by a disease, possibly typhoid, supposedly emanating from the well

of Kairikelda, which had caused the island to be abandoned. So now its only inhabitants are birds and the occasional visiting naturalist.

Most of the islanders had lived in a tight huddle of buildings near the south end of Eynhallow. A strange life it must have been, living on top of each other, dependent on the bare, flattish island and the sea for sustenance, with the rest of the world so close and clearly visible but so often out of reach. After their departure the settlement was fired, presumably to prevent the survivors returning and being exposed to disease again. Only then, when the roofs, staircases and partitions had been burnt off and the bare stone revealed, was it realised that the three dwellings in the centre of the huddle had occupied the chancel, nave and porch of an ancient church, whose very existence had been long forgotten. It is thought that this was the long lost Norse monastery of Orkney, though the present buildings are probably twelfth century.

Orkney. The island monastery of Eynhallow.

The ruins were measured and drawn in 1866 by H. Dryden, and in 1897 the site was cleared and consolidated by William Lethaby, the Arts and Crafts architect of Melsetter House on Hoy. This is what we see today. Lethaby also built the corrugated iron lodge now used by naturalists.

The monastic church which now stood revealed was a solidly built three-cell structure with fine arches between its component parts. A fireplace and chimney had been contrived at the east end, domestic doorways and windows knocked through, and an upper floor inserted, but otherwise it was pretty complete. A square outshut on the south side of the nave houses a substantial turning stair of stone. Where did it lead to? The line of the roof seems to preclude any connection with the upper floor which had been contrived in the nave. It brings to mind the island monastery of Inchcolm, in the Firth of Forth, where the tiny cloister is built on two levels.

▲ **Above**: *The church interior of Eynhallow was lost for centuries in a huddle of dwellings.*

▶ **Right**: *Chapel Barn, Suffolk, in its long years as a barn.*

CHAPEL BARN, BURES, SUFFOLK

It is a quiet out-of-the-way place near the Suffolk–Essex border, at the end of a dirt track, looking out over a wide, shallow valley, but it has seen high drama. On this spot on Christmas Day 855, Edmund, aged fifteen and of the old Saxon race, was crowned king by Humbert, Bishop of Elmham. In 869 Edmund led an army against the Vikings, but was defeated and captured by them. Refusing to renounce his Christian faith, he was shot full of arrows and then beheaded. In about 915 his uncorrupted body was brought to Bury St Edmunds, where King Athelstan founded a small community of priests to care for his shrine. As the cult of St Edmund burgeoned so this grew into one of the greatest abbeys in the land, surrounded by a prosperous town. Edmund, king and martyr, became a patron saint of England. He is superbly depicted on the exquisite Wilton Diptych, made for Richard II between 1395 and 1399 and now in the National Gallery, London. St Edmund with his arrow, Edward the Confessor with his ring, and John the Baptist in rags are presenting the young and kneeling king to Mary and the infant Jesus, surrounded by a host of angels. St Edmund is remembered at the many churches dedicated to him, especially in East Anglia.

On St Stephen's Day, 26 December 1218, a chapel was consecrated by Stephen Langton, Archbishop of Canterbury, to commemorate the place of Edmund's coronation. The painted consecration marks can still be seen. It was a simple but elegant building in the Early English style, of rendered flint, with five bays of lancets. A light thatched roof in the East Anglian way made buttresses unnecessary.

The Old Chapel Bures

J S Corder 1901

By about 1500 the chapel was deserted, its origin forgotten and lost to sight. Too good a building to waste, it was turned into a row of cottages for a while and then into a useful barn. The west wall was knocked out and it was lengthened to a barn shape with a timber-framed extension. A pair of broad wagon doors was knocked out through the middle, one on each side. The windows were blocked up and ventilation holes opened up under the eaves. Filled with corn, or piled high with mangelwurzels, it looked much like any other barn. It was even used as an isolation hospital for a while. Only its name remained.

So it stood for four centuries, a workaday building muddy and battered, until in 1931 the neighbouring house was bought by Isabel Badcock, and she and her brother-in-law, Geoffrey Probert, took the chapel in hand. Together they rescued and restored it over the next decade. The roof was rethatched, the west wall rebuilt, lancet windows reopened. The wagon doors were removed and the gaping holes rebuilt, with a new south door and window. The interior was fitted out chapel-wise with a motley but rich collection of furnishings.

In 1935 Chapel Barn was made more magnificent than it ever was before, though this introduced an element of false history, by bringing in three splendid de Vere tomb chests with their alabaster effigies which were looking for a home. They are the 5th (d. 1296), 8th (d. 1371) and 11th (d. 1412) Earls of Oxford, plus the 11th's countess. These have had their own adventures. Originally in Colne Priory in Essex, they were removed at the dissolution into the parish church, then in 1827 to a modern priory – each time being altered to fit. Now, reconstructed as far as possible, they rest here.

Chapel Barn was reconsecrated in 1940, a year after Isabel Badcock died. She is buried outside, against the sunny south wall; and so, now, is Geoffrey Probert. The restored chapel stands in the gentle countryside with a single house and their two graves for company.

◀ **Left**: *Chapel Barn. Piled with beets or mangelwurzels, its distinguished origin forgotten.*

▼ **Overleaf**: *Chapel Barn, restored today to more than its original glory.*

CHAPTER 4

DROWNED, SWEPT AWAY,
BURIED ALIVE

~

MARDALE, DERWENT, NORMANTON, MELVERLEY

Manchester has ever been thirsty for clean water. The gritty city gets plenty of rain, but the Industrial Revolution fatally sullied its rivers. The Lake District is even wetter, and still pristine. In the 1890s Manchester's Thirlmere scheme linked the two together, bringing seemingly limitless clean water a hundred miles from the Lakes to the city. It was an engineering marvel, requiring only gravity to fetch the waters. Along with the opening of the Manchester Ship Canal in 1894 it marked a high point in the city's fortunes. Not without controversy, however, because the enlarged Thirlmere drowned one of the Lake District's celebrated landscapes. The old Thirlmere had narrowed to a point in the middle where a chain of three little packhorse bridges could cross. Poetically dwarfed by the surrounding mountains, the scene was a favourite with artists and early photographers alike. Now all that was gone. Although resistance to the scheme had proved futile in the end, it gave rise to a concerted effort for the future preservation of the Lakeland landscape. The whole conservation movement grew out of this and similar issues.

A generation later Manchester was still thirsty. This time its gaze focused on the small northern lake of Haweswater. The scheme to turn it into a reservoir, much bigger than the original lake, was authorised in 1919.

As at Thirlmere, there was an influx of hundreds of navvies and their families. They were housed in a temporary village at Burnbanks, and their children swelled the class numbers at Bampton school. The village churches of Mardale and Bampton saw extra activity. But Bampton was below the dam, and the village and church survive. Mardale was above, and was doomed. Its church was a small building of rough stone with a low west tower, no doubt once whitewashed. Like the churches at Buttermere and Wasdale Head, its humble simplicity seemed absolutely right in such magnificent surroundings.

The last service in the little church of Mardale on 18 August 1935 was crowded out. Hundreds stood in the field as the service was relayed on loudspeakers. Then it was demolished. A few of the dressed stones were used in the castellated straining well of the reservoir. Nearly 100 bodies were disinterred from the churchyard and reburied at Shap. The old Dun Bull Inn was demolished, to be replaced by the unlovely Haweswater Hotel. As the dam was completed the water

◄ **Previous page**: *The little church of Mardale receives one last pilgrim.*

► **This page**: *The steeple of the drowned Derwent Church was allowed to remain for a few years, providing a new wonder of the Peak.*

level started to rise. Mardale was no more.

The drowning of Mardale is not entirely forgotten or forgiven even now. The church was not in itself remarkable, and the greatly enlarged Haweswater might even be thought more beautiful in its way than the old lake. So why the fuss?

Stand at the head of Haweswater on a fine morning, looking over the site of the village, and you can begin to understand. Mardale was, to borrow a phrase of Thomas Gray, a little unsuspected paradise. A natural arbour at the head of the valley, green and fertile, it was removed from the busy world by the high fells on three sides, and on the fourth by the stillness of the undisturbed lake. Peace and plenty in the midst of untamed grandeur, the very image of the beautiful and the sublime. Manchester's gain – and we can never underestimate the benefits of clean water – was undoubtedly a loss for the rest of us.

A similar tale – but with a twist – unfolded a few years later in the Peak District of Derbyshire. Sheffield's thirst was almost equal to Manchester's, and the city's natural water supply lay closer to hand, in the Peak District. There was no natural lake, but the very long and deep but narrow branching valley of the Derwent offered good potential for water storage. The first two reservoirs were created in 1906–16. Their dams exhibit magnificent Victorian-style engineering, dressed in rock-faced stone and punctuated by towers. The site was made famous by the trial runs carried out by Lancaster bombers before the Dam Busters raid in May 1943. It is a strange place today, wild and yet unnatural with its big dripping conifers and bare waterline, depopulated and yet full of people – cyclists, walkers, teenagers with giant rucksacks on Duke of Edinburgh Award hikes, RAF recruits come to view the Dam Busters memorial.

The lowest and biggest reservoir, Ladybower, with its earth-faced dam was not built until 1935–45. The A57 Snake Pass crosses it on a concrete viaduct. It was this that led to the drowning of Derwent church and manor. The church of Sts James and John was carefully dismantled, its stone and furnishings distributed to Hathersage church and elsewhere. This time, however, the tower and broach spire of the church were allowed to remain, at least for a while.

The steeple was an amazing sight poking out of the rising waters, like the tower of Orthanc at the end of *The Lord of the Rings*. Far more dramatic than the church had ever been in life, it attracted much more attention, especially when the water was drawn down and you could wade across to it. Officialdom became alarmed, quoting safety concerns, and on 15 December 1947 it was dynamited and destroyed. A real pity; this was a sight to see, briefly one of the wonders of the Peak.

The creation of Rutland Water is a more recent affair. A vast but shallow reservoir, almost an inland sea, supplying water to Peterborough and Leicester, it started to fill in the 1970s. This time it was the classical estate church of Normanton that was doomed.

The landed estate of Normanton (13,600 acres) had been sold in 1924. The great house, having failed to reach its reserve, was stripped, burnt out and then demolished. The old village in the manner of the time had already been cleared away to improve the view, but the church was left. It had been rebuilt classical in 1764 and in 1826 had gained a sophisticated circular tower and portico.

The next problem was what to do with it. Several rescue options were canvassed. It could be moved bodily, like the church at Most (see chapter 6), to a new site above the water. It could be jacked up, as the Shambles was in Manchester, and raised above the waters. Or it could be dismantled and rebuilt elsewhere. In the end it was left *in situ*, filled in with rubble to the requisite height and made the centrepiece of an artificial island linked to the mainland by a causeway. Half drowned, in fact. It does look odd, seeming to float upon the choppy waters but at the same time to be for ever sinking, like the Barcaccia Fountain in Piazza di Spagna in Rome, but when you stand in the semicircular portico at its prow it could almost be a Greek temple in the midst of the Ionian Sea.

Now a new use was needed. It functioned as an unsatisfactory museum for a while, but today, following many requests, it has become a venue for civil weddings. And very romantic it must be, the interior pure white and filled with reflections from the water outside, the portico worthy of Greece itself, with the waves breaking on the rocks at your very feet.

Normanton Church in its ancestral parkland, before the creation of Rutland Water.

So, by popular demand the church of St Matthew at Normanton has reverted to something like its age-old function. A place to celebrate rites of passage, and an unexpectedly satisfactory outcome.

Melverley church in Shropshire illustrates a different story. In fact there is no story as yet, but the church stands on the brink. This time it is not a man-made reservoir that threatens it but the River Vyrynwy. The river is normally docile enough, but like the Herefordshire bull in the next field it can turn nasty, and then there is no stopping it. The river can rise alarmingly, as it did during the 1990 Flower Festival when a thunderstorm raged all around, and then it seemed as though the whole church could be washed away into the mighty Severn, which the Vyrynwy joins just round the corner, and out to sea. In fact the river bank had to be strengthened with a massive steel piling operation shortly afterwards.

Melverley church is a special case, however, for it would float. It is a rare black and white church, framed and pegged in oak. It is a fine example of timber-framing in the local style, exactly sixteen paces long and eight wide. The north wall with just one tiny window makes an especially impressive display of close studding. Theoretically, therefore, it would not be difficult to dismantle the whole thing and rebuild elsewhere – the timbers are already numbered in readiness.

THE LEGENDARY CITY OF DUNWICH

Every winter our coasts are battered by the sea. On the rocky south and west coasts the repeated gales of January 2014 sent huge waves and tidal surges to overtop harbour walls and demolish immemorial rock arches. Brunel's railway at Dawlish, the only remaining rail link with Plymouth and Cornwall, was breached. On the east coast, from Kent up to Lincolnshire and beyond, North Sea waves chew at the low clayey cliffs, undermining them until the last thing to hold the land together is the close-cropped turf on top. It cannot last. Cracks appear and soon another chunk will go sliding and crashing down on to the beach below.

Whole towns have disappeared this way, the most celebrated being Dunwich in Suffolk. It is difficult to separate fact from legend, but here was once a whole thriving town and port, with the best harbour in East Anglia, a flourishing trade and several shipyards, nine parish churches and three chapels, two friaries and two hospitals; all swallowed up by the sea. It was notorious until 1832 as the rottenest of the rotten boroughs, still sending two MPs to parliament long after the town had gone. Today the place is deserted; just a few cottages, a long sweep of shingle, low, crumbling cliffs and the distant tower of Southwold remind us of what was once here.

One by one the landmarks of the town yielded to the impetuosity of the billows, as *The Beauties of England and Wales* (1813) so poetically puts it. Several churches were lost in a great storm in 1286, and in 1327 the port was rendered useless as the Dunwich River changed its course. Four hundred houses together with shops and windmills had gone by 1350, along with the churches of St Leonard, St Martin and

Dunwich. The surviving gateway of the Greyfriars.

Dunwich, The ruins of All Saints in an early engraving.

St Nicholas. The dead were washed from their graves; skeletons were found scattered on the beach. The sea reached the marketplace in 1677, and in 1702 St Peter's church and the town hall were lost. In 1715 even the jail had to be abandoned. By 1832, when the Reform Act finally did away with its representation in parliament, there were forty-four houses left and just thirty-two voters. The last church to go was All Saints. Still complete in 1750, it had been stripped by 1776. By 1886 the sea had reached the east end and in 1904 it had started to topple over. The last part of the nave had gone over by 1919, and later that year the tower fell, excepting one buttress – which has been rebuilt as a relic by the new church of St James.

The Franciscan friary stood inland, outside town. Its perimeter wall is now just twelve paces from the hungry sea, and clearly has not long to go, although in 2013 it was rather forlornly being repaired by Suffolk County Council. Not far away, and sensibly built outside town, is a remnant of the leper hospital of St James. A ruined Norman apse with arcading, which must have been very fine, stands next to the modern parish church. This modest church has its own peculiar story – in its way another lost church. It was originally built of white brick in the classical style in 1830, with pilasters and a circular cupola, something like Normanton church in Rutland, by architect Robert Appleton. But by 1845 such a 'pagan' style was out of fashion, and it was Gothicked to make it look more churchy. Flint was applied to the walls, the cupola raised into a thin tower, the windows made pointed, an open roof substituted for the comfortable ceiling. So the classical church, now the only church of Dunwich, disappeared, and a Gothic one took its place.

COVEHITHE

A few miles to the north is Covehithe. Like Dunwich, this was once a flourishing place. Now there is just a single farm, a ruined church and a road leading, literally, to nowhere. Past the church the lane ends abruptly in a barrier, DANGER notices and a tangle of brambles. Beyond, the waves crash on to the beach below. Walkers are warned to keep clear of the collapsing cliffs, and overhangs held together merely by the soil and turf on top underline the danger.

Enough remains of St Andrew's church to show that it was once splendid, of noble size and fine proportions, with a two-storey porch and tall six-bay arcades. We can visualise something as grand as St Edmund's in Southwold, with an angel roof maybe and a painted rood loft and screen. Now the wind blows through the gaping windows, and a robin nests in the crumbling masonry. A humble little thatched church, cobbled up in 1672 when the big church was abandoned, shelters in the ruins, adding extra poignancy to the scene. The sea gets ever closer, the sandy cliffs collapsing with every storm and taking the lane and the fields with it. It cannot be long before the whole thing tumbles into the sea, like Dunwich.

This page: Covehithe. The shell of the grand church stands, with its humble successor of 1672 huddling inside – but for how much longer?

RECULVER

The loss of the ancient Saxon minster of St Mary at Reculver in Kent, founded by St Augustine himself, is most grievous and tantalising, because it survived intact for so long, and because its destruction was, as it turned out, unnecessary.

Augustine, sent out from Rome by Pope Gregory in the year 596 as a missionary to the pagan Angles, angels, or English, landed with a small band of brothers upon Thanet, then an island, at the north-east tip of Kent. The Roman fort of Reculver, or Regulbium, guarded the north end of the channel called Wantsum, which divided Thanet from the mainland; the better preserved fort of Richborough, or Rutupieae, is at the other end. Negotiations with King Ethelbert were eventually successful, many were baptised, and in due course Augustine founded the future cathedrals of Canterbury, Rochester and London. At Reculver he established a monastery within the walls of the fort. Its church was cross-shaped, with a broad nave separated from a wide apse by a tripartite arched screen carried upon a pair of tall columns, as was also to be found at Bradwell in Essex. In front of the screen stood a magnificently carved stone cross.

This is John Leland's account, written in the 1530s/1540s:

Yn the enteryng of the quyer ys one of the fayrest, and the most auncyent crosse that ever I saw, a IX footes as I ges, yn highte. Yt standeth like a fayr columne. The base great stone is not wrought. The second stone being round hath curiusly wrought and paynted the images of Christ, Peter, Paule, John and James, as I remember. Christ sayeth Ego sum Alpha et Omega. Peter sayeth Tu es Christus filius Deo vovi. The saing of the other iii wher painted majusculus literis Ro. but now obliterated. The second stone is of the passion. The iii conteineth the xi Apostles. The iiii hath the image of Christ hanging and fastened by iiii nayles, and sub pedibus sustentaculum. The hiest part of the pyller hath the figure of a crosse.

Over the years the church's apse was squared off, and it acquired a pair of bold western towers with matching broach spires. It made a fine sight on the

low cliff top, and an excellent navigational aid for mariners. Within, however, the ancient church was essentially intact.

So it stood until 1809, when the whole lot was demolished apart from the twin towers. The parish clerk records: 'Mr C.C. Nailor been Vicar of the parish, his mother fancied that the church was kept for a poppet show, and she persuaded her son to take it down.'

Perhaps this is a little unfair. The guide to the present church tells a more nuanced tale.

In 1807 the sea, which had already taken half the Roman fort and reduced the village to a few cottages, had reached to within a few feet of the north tower of the church. There seemed no hope of saving it. 'Planking and piling' was put in, but to no avail. In 1808 the parish council passed a resolution, carried by one vote and including that of the vicar, Christopher Bramble Naylor, to demolish the church. Permission was sought from the Archbishop of Canterbury. His appointed commission recommended that the rapid approach of the sea made it absolutely

◀ **Opposite page**: *Reculver. The twin towers of the ancient church were preserved as a seamark, but the rest needlessly demolished.*

▲ **Above**: *The modern church of Reculver, provided at one remove to replace the Saxon minster.*

necessary, so that the materials could be saved for a new church on a safer site. Consent was given, and in 1809 the venerable church came down.

At the last minute Trinity House stepped in to buy the twin towers as an aid to navigation. They built stone groynes on the beach below to preserve them, and these, plus possibly a change in the ocean currents, have done the trick, effectively halting the erosion. The site is still intact. So the ancient minster could have been saved after all.

Following the demolition of the old minster a new church was built on a safer site, using the rubble and spoil from the old one. This must have been a poor construction, because in 1878 it had to be demolished and rebuilt again. This is the church we see today, a standard Victorian building with a few old stones in its chancel arch. Four or five pieces of intricately carved work, presumably part of the ancient cross, were saved and preserved in the crypt of Canterbury Cathedral, though even these are not currently on show. The two columns of the screen were also preserved. Otherwise everything is lost.

The destruction of the Reculver cross is particularly grievous because it was the only one of its kind known in the south of England, except perhaps the two 'pyramids' seen by Leland at Glastonbury but also now vanished. The only comparable pieces are in the far north, at Bewcastle in Cumberland and Ruthwell in Dumfriesshire, although the Reculver Cross, unlike them, was cylindrical. The surviving fragments and Leland's description conjure up a highly accomplished piece, carved and coloured with figures of Roman dignity. Like all such pieces there is much antiquarian controversy about the date, but it is possible that the cross was here first and the church built around it.

The scene has changed today. The north-east tip of Kent is considerably industrialised: railways, roads, power lines, airport are much in evidence. The Wantsum dried up long ago, so Thanet is no longer an island. However, rising sea levels could mean that this may not be permanent – its banks are being piled against flooding at Sandwich. While Reculver has been half eaten up by the sea, Richborough is now high and dry, a long way back from the present

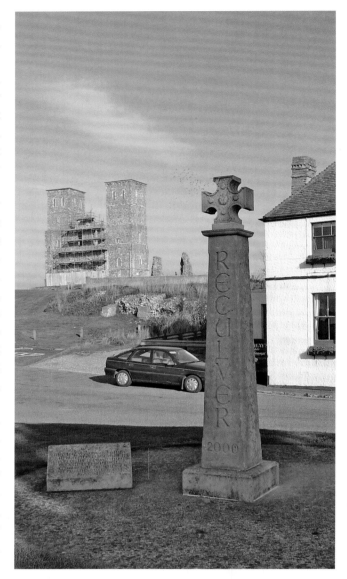

shoreline. The twin towers of Reculver stand proud but are flat-topped, having lost their spires. The foundations of the rest of the church are clear and rise quite high at the corners of the squared-off chancel. The rounded apse and the position of the two columns of the screen are marked on the ground. Many Saxon coins of the time have been discovered round the church.

A new Reculver Cross was put up in front of the King Ethelbert Inn for the millennium. It is a poor effort, not round but conventionally square, with nothing written upon it but Reculver 2000. How little we have to say compared with our ancestors.

◀ **Opposite page**: *Reculver.*
The millennium cross.

▲ *Above: Perranzabuloe. The*
pool and all that is left of the
oratory in the sands.

PERRANZABULOE, OR ST PIRAN'S IN THE SANDS, CORNWALL

In about the year 450 St Piran, who by his incessant preaching and holy example had irritated the king of Ireland beyond endurance, was thrown into the sea. With a millstone round his neck, so they say. He was cast up on the north coast of Cornwall upon the vast windswept expanse of Penhale Sands. Parched and starving, he pulled his boat clear of the surf and staggered up into the inhospitable dunes. There he found a sheltered hollow and a miraculous pool of clear fresh water. By the pool he built himself a shelter. Perhaps it was of wood, though there is none except what the sea might cast up (I found none). Perhaps of stones picked off the beach. Or maybe simply of his upturned coracle. At all events an oratory or prayer-house was built, of stones set in mud from the pool and thatched with the harsh grass of the sand dunes. It was 25 feet long by 12 feet inside, with

a doorway in the side towards the pool and another in the corner by the altar. Carved faces, man, woman and 'tyger', decorated the doorway. A tiny window, or perhaps two, gave a little extra light. A stone seat ran round the inside walls. Here the curious came to hear what Piran had to say, and those that believed were baptised in the pool.

This is an idyllic place on a rare calm day, but in a storm the dunes shift and blow with the wind. The whole shape of the landscape can change overnight. St Piran's oratory had to be dug out so many times that it was allowed to stay buried. A church was built nearby on higher and more stable ground, next to a stone cross. Even that was not safe from the drifting sand, and it was eventually replaced by a church in Perranporth.

In the year 1835 an extra big blow temporarily uncovered St Piran's little oratory. It caused great excitement, being hailed as perhaps the earliest Christian building in the country. Descriptions and measured drawings were published in the learned journals of the day.

Unfortunately St Piran's has been an archaeological disaster ever since. Walls built of stones set in mud will stand just so long as they have a good roof to protect them, or are buried in sand, but when exposed to the weather and the feet of the curious they simply fall down. The little building fell to bits, the carved stones of the doorways disappeared. Something had to be done before it disintegrated completely. In 1910 a block and concrete bunker was built over the whole thing. A bold inscription declared SANCTUS PIRANUS IN ZABULO, but otherwise it made things worse – a big mistake. As well as being ugly, it filled with water. A report of 1978 was sharply critical, describing the remains as 'mostly a very bad 20th-century rebuild, held up by a clumsy concrete corset, excavated to below footing level and devoid of any features or details'. In 1980 the bunker was unroofed and the whole caboodle was buried in sand again.

Even though there was nothing to be seen, the site remained important to the Cornish. St Piran's Day in March is a big event. A tall concrete cross was put up on a dune nearby, forming the focus of the annual celebrations. A play is declaimed in the Cornish language and, weather permitting, Piran himself lands upon the sands once more.

In 2014 the site was opened up again. Enclosed by the remaining courses of the bunker, the pathetic remnants of St Piran's oratory are now

▲ Opposite page above: A festive gathering at St Piran's in the early twentieth century showing the protective shed under construction.

◀ Opposite page: St. Piran. Excavation of the fragile ruins.

◀ Left: St Piran. Not the finest moment in recent archaeological history.

draped in plastic and sandbags. A big pile of excavated sand has been dumped nearby, tipped over the military fence that encloses so much of the dunes.

The story of St Piran and his oratory in the sands is not a happy one, but it has an unexpected sequel. Far away in Cumberland, Sara Losh of Wreay was excited by the original accounts of the discovery. A true product of the Enlightenment, Sara Losh was a remarkable woman. She is known chiefly for the astonishingly original church she built at Wreay in 1842, but her antiquarian recreations deserve their place in history as well. Always interested in the antique, she determined to build her own early Christian chapel. Taking the reported dimensions of St Piran's oratory and the disposition of the two doors and window, she built a mortuary chapel next to the cemetery plot she had given to her village. Three faces were carved for each door – man, woman and tyger. The stone bench, the stone altar, the unsplayed window – all are faithfully reproduced. But it is built of good Cumbrian stone, properly coursed and bedded in mortar, and roofed in stone. The door jambs are true and vertical, the arches turned in the fashionable basket shape. Most tellingly, the carved faces cannot help taking on the neo-Classical look (see those Roman noses) of the 1830s. You can never really free yourself of your own time and style.

▼ **Below**: *At Wreay in Cumberland, Sara Losh built a replica of the then (1835) newly discovered oratory of St Piran.*

▶ **Opposite page**: *St Enodoc. The church, excavated from the drifting dunes, still looks half-buried.*

ST ENODOC

The north Cornish coast is a favourite holiday place today, and has been ever since the Southern Railway arrived at Wadebridge and Padstow. 'Oh, the days of the Atlantic Coast Express: Can it really be that this same carriage came from Waterloo?'

John Betjeman first holidayed here as a child in 1910, and he returned every year. He loved the place, the tides, the waves, the butterflies and the scent of thyme, the golf links and the holidaymakers, and remembered it fondly in his poetry and blank verse. Of St Enodoc he wrote:

> What faith was his, that dim, that Cornish saint,
> Small rushlight of a long-forgotten church,
> Who lived with God on this unfriendly shore,
> Who knew He made the Atlantic and the stones
> And destined seamen here to end their lives
> Dashed on a rock, rolled over in the surf,
> And not one hair forgotten.

Many will remember the poet and broadcaster's boshed golf shot on TV – 'and ... missed it!' – and the huge laugh that followed. His mother is buried here, and so is Betjeman himself, his grave marked by a slate gravestone extravagantly scrolled.

Golfers and dogwalkers in the dunes above Daymer Bay are treated to the unlikely sight of a dumpy church spire, endearingly wonky, apparently poking straight out of the ground. Notices warn of flying golf balls, but they also highlight attempts to stabilise the fragile dunes. In a stiff breeze this can be seen to be a real problem, as the surface of the loose sand stirs in constant motion. Come a big blow and the whole shape of the dunes can change, blowing out in one place and piling high in another. By the beginning of the nineteenth century the church of St Enodoc was lost, buried in the sand, with only its spire and gable tops to mark its position. The vicar had to be lowered in through a hole in the roof in order to say the yearly service that prevented its legal abandonment.

The church was finally rescued and dug out in 1864, the walls and windows cleared, the churchyard turfed and the church path cut through. You can still sit on a bench in the churchyard looking down upon its roofs, and blown sand has to be cleared away regularly.

An additional surprise it is to find in the church a monument to three latter-day mariners who lost their lives in a shipwreck. Emily Macfarlane, John Shannon and Anne Taylor died in 1995 when the restored 1858 brig *Maria Asumpta* was lost on the rocks. Their beautiful memorial was carved by Philip Chatfield, who had also been on the ship when she was wrecked.

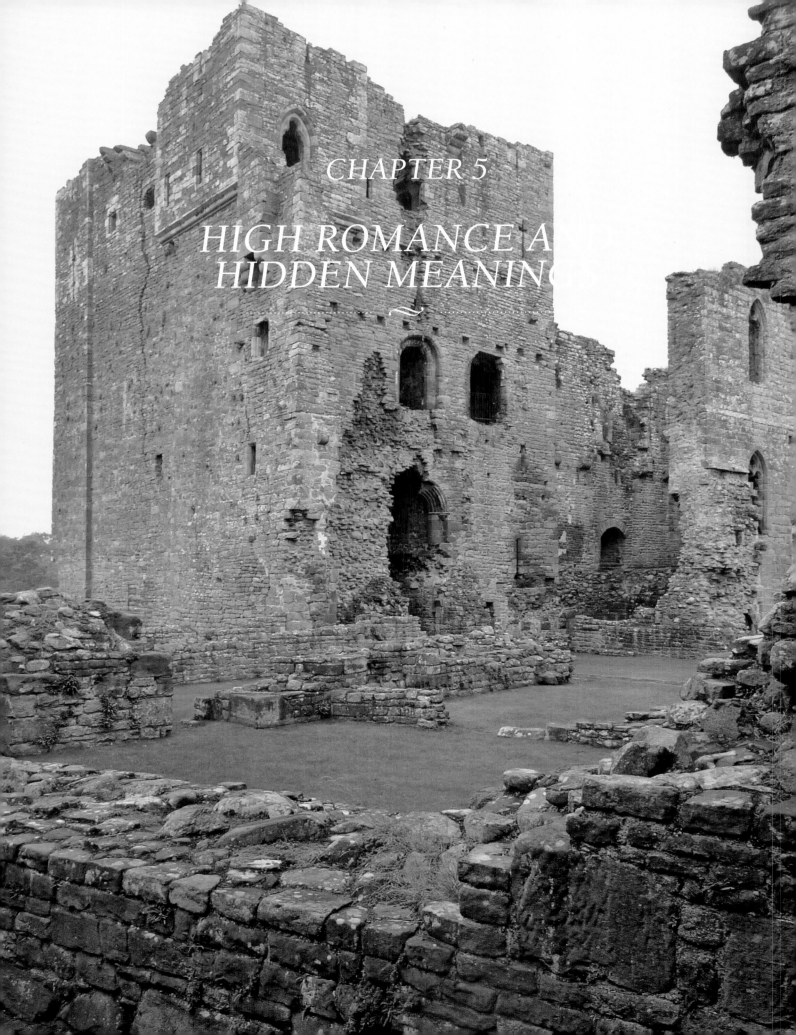

CHAPTER 5

HIGH ROMANCE A
HIDDEN MEANIN

THE CASTLE ORATORY AT BROUGHAM, WESTMORLAND

The castle of Brougham, just across the river from Penrith, is as grim and comfortless as most castles. The walls rise sheer above the river crossing it was built to guard. The Eamont, which flows from Ullswater and out into the River Eden, was an important boundary. Concentrated in form, the castle was built on a corner of its predecessor Roman fort and no doubt cannibalises a good many of its stones.

The approach is not friendly. A frowning gatehouse with its iron portcullis and watchful guardhouse leads to a dark passageway, its vault punctuated by murder holes. This emerges not into the castle bailey but into a claustrophobic courtyard commanded on all sides by threatening arrowslits. A truly murderous space if you had no business to be there. A second gatehouse and passage follows, and only then are you in the main open courtyard of the castle. This is a wide and stony space, paved with waterwashed stones from the river, hard underfoot. It is easy to imagine the clatter of horses' hooves and jingle of harnesses echoing round the stone walls that surround it. Stables, lodgings, brewhouse and kitchens line the outer walls, with the hall and attendant chapel above; all are pretty ruinous now. Towering sheer and almost windowless above it all is the great Norman keep. Such is the odd design of Brougham that you have to go round almost a complete circuit before you can enter.

Entry to the keep is on the first floor, above vaulted cellars, and protected by a defensive forebuilding. The lower floors are functional, oppressed by the immensely thick walls and poorly lit, but high above them, indeed above everything else, is a place of high romance. The big octagonal room that occupied the topmost floor of the keep, removed from the martial hurly-burly of the castle, stood for a more civilised life. It has gone, along with all the floors and roofs, but there is enough left to reconstruct it. It was well lit from deep-embrasured windows on all four sides and warmed by a generous fireplace in one corner. Each embrasure was equipped with window seats and a ribbed arch above, like a little room-with-a-room. The walls were probably painted and hung with tapestry.

Encircling this great room, and looking out though slit windows over the rest of the castle and the wide country beyond, is a passageway built in the thickness of the wall and roofed with stone slabs. The passage widens out in one corner to take the turning stair that leads up from the rest of the castle, and which continues up to the wall walks and turrets overhead. In the south-east corner, in one of those astonishing works of intricate beauty the fourteenth-century masons occasionally delighted in, is a tiny chapel. The whole thing has been fitted into a tiny and awkward space, but everything needful is there. A doorway in the south side of the great room leads to a preparatory passage, a sort of narthex, lit by its own window and lined with a pair of arched recesses on each side. Perhaps they were for books. Its window is angled to look down at the main castle chapel below. A cusped archway leads into the chapel proper. Even in ruination this is a most exquisite space. A traceried window above the altar faces due east, towards the

◀ **Left**: *Brougham Castle. The chapel or oratory perches high up at the top of the keep.*

▼ **Below**: *Still romantic in ruin. The keep chapel of Brougham.*

sunrise and Jerusalem. To the right is recessed an arched piscina, for the washing of holy vessels, and to the left an aumbry, or cupboard, for the bread and wine. To the left of the altar and aumbry a small door leads into a tiny sacristy, where the priest would robe up, with a built-in cupboard in which to keep the sacred vessels for the mass. A domed vault arches overhead, its ribs meeting in a round boss carved with two faces.

This is a kind of non-space, out of the world, only existing in the thickness of the wall. We are conscious of three floors of solid masonry underfoot, and solid stone above, and yet it has a grace and lightness quite apart from the rest of the castle.

The colour has gone, the glass and tracery from the window are no more. There is no glint of gold or silver or sheen of precious fabric. No candles burn steadily through the night upon the altar slab, no knight lies prostrate on the floor in vigil before setting out on pilgrimage, or riding out into battle. Only an owl sits upon the gaping windowsill and hoots into the moonlit night below.

KNOWLTON CHURCH AND HENGE, DORSET

The wide downlands of Wiltshire and Dorset are rich in the great works of our Stone Age ancestors. This is magnificent country, wide open to the skies and offering vast views in all directions. Here at Knowlton in Dorset is a Neolithic henge. A lowish grass bank encloses a ditch on the inside (proving that it was not defensive) and a big circle of flat turf. Bank and ditch are interrupted for a clear entrance to the south-west. On the opposite north-eastern perimeter, close together, are the wrecks of two ancient yew trees. A hundred yards or so away to the south-east is a high mound. Aerial photographs show that this had its own circular ditch at some distance. Two other henges in the group are now only visible from the air: a smaller one to the north-west, and a bigger one, now bisected by the road and a farm, to the south. There is nothing else.

Except that bang in the middle of Knowlton henge is a church. Humble and long ruined, it yet stands alone in the vast empty landscape, offered up on the grass amphitheatre of the henge like a cake on a

▲ **Above left & right**: *Knowlton church and henge. The high mount or tumulus throws a long shadow, and the ghost of a second henge surrounds the farm.*

◀ **Left**: *Knowlton. Not much is left of the body of the church, but the striped tower stands almost complete.*

cake plate. The low tower of striped brown stone and flint is missing only its floors and parapets. The rest is more ruinous; a small roofless nave and chancel, and on the north side a little chapel and a narrow aisle. The doorway and chancel arch are simplest Norman. An ornamented bracket in the corner of the chapel could have held an image or statue. There is not much more that can be said.

'The henge may have served some ceremonial purpose', reads the English Heritage board in the vaguest possible terms. There can have been nothing vague about the impulse that motivated our Neolithic ancestors to set out great astronomical circles and to dig, with nothing but deer antlers and flint and wood, great ditches and mounds in the harsh chalky ground. In any case, how long will it be before the same vague statement can be made about the church? We have already forgotten its dedication, and the reason for building it exactly there. And where are the communities that built these things, both the henge and the church?

It may be that the church was built in order to neutralise the henge. Perhaps it covers something of deep significance to the early peoples of the area. We cannot know, and because the church is there it is the one place that cannot be excavated by the archaeologists. It was a wise policy of the early church not to obliterate the old sacred sites but simply take them over. Sometimes, however, they seemed to retain a power that the church was not able to control. Maybe it was this that led to the destruction of many of the standing stones at Avebury. The building and position of a church could defuse the situation. At Stanton Drew in Somerset, where three stone circles almost intersect, the village church was built in such a way as to block the link between the cove and the circles, depriving the complex of its coherence. The huge pattern of the Neolithic complex can only now be appreciated in a diagram or air view.

Curiously, and despite all first impressions, Knowlton is not dead. A candle stub stands in a crevice of the chancel stonework, and there has evidently been a small fire where the altar once stood. The two ancient yew trees on the perimeter bank prove to be active shrines, bedecked with ribbons and flags and decorated in every crack and cranny with votive objects. What muddled religion or mysticism survives in this remote, long-abandoned, yet still powerful place?

A walk over the field to the mound throws up another puzzle. It is a great barrow, a burial place of long ago, and still impressively high. Rabbits appear to love it, and the whole thing is riddled with their burrows and the white chalk they have dug out. It makes one realise how startling the henge and its ditch must have looked when freshly dug and dazzling white. Tree-covered until recently, all those on the barrow have been trashed and broken, leaving it open to be eroded by the

▲ **Above**: *Knowlton church and henge from the distant mount. The two ancient yews on the far right are still hallowed after a fashion.*

▶ **Right**: *Rosslyn Chapel at dusk.*

elements. Why? Is this the result of some storm, or a latter-day manifestation of the enmity towards the ancient sacred sites that led our recent ancestors to expend so much energy in pulling down the stones of Avebury?

▲ **Above**: *Rosslyn. The vaulting of the retro-choir and the famous apprentice pillars.*

ROSSLYN CHAPEL

Churches can become famous for the oddest of reasons. In the case of Rosslyn it was a work of pulp fiction: Dan Brown's *The Da Vinci Code*, published in 2003. To be fair, though, the Collegiate Chapel of St Matthew at Rosslyn, near Edinburgh, is extraordinary enough in its own right.

Among the wealthy lairds of fifteenth- and sixteenth-century Scotland there was quite a fashion for founding a collegiate church. A place where your sins, which might be many, could be expiated and where your soul, which might be in dire need of salvation, could be prayed for in perpetuity. In 1446, or it might have been 1450, Sir William St Clair, third and last Prince of Orkney, founded a collegiate church at Rosslyn, a few miles south of Edinburgh. He wanted it to outshine all the others, in fact every other church in Scotland, not by its great size – it is quite tiny – but in the overpowering richness of its decoration and the strange meanings that it might enshrine.

In his travels Sir William appears to have collected examples he wanted to copy. The plan of his chapel reproduces that of the choir of Glasgow Cathedral, but on a miniature scale. The double flying buttresses of Melrose Abbey must have impressed him, so here they are, though they are without function and there is barely room to squeeze them in. It may be that he had seen a decorated and patterned vault somewhere (Portugal maybe?), and so he had his master mason apply a pattern of raised blocks upon the Scottish tunnel vault that crowns his church. Or it may be that his mason came from an exotic land. We cannot know. And what was the inspiration for the slightly obscene bosses that hang down from the false ribs of the vault, or those that protrude almost at eye level in the Lady Chapel?

Structurally speaking the chapel is very odd, and would never stand up if it was any bigger. The aisles are spanned by flat stone lintels, strictly flat arches, highly decorated like everything else but structurally dubious. Admittedly the vault that apparently rests upon them is also slightly arched, taking some of the weight off, but it only works because of its small scale. The high vault is a pointed tunnel, whose weight will always try to push out the walls that carry it. The impressive looking flying buttresses can do little to resist this because they only bear at certain points. The only way is to make the supporting walls thick. Raising it up on a clerestory with big windows, as it is here, is a risky procedure. The thin stone of the vault itself is all there is between the chapel and the Scottish weather. There is no separate roof above it, and no air space, so its curved shape shows outside.

A subterranean stair leads down from the east end of the chapel to a dark, vaulted sacristy. This is a sizeable room but dark and mysterious, part buried in the hillside. It is recorded that the 2nd Earl directed that he should be buried in the family crypt that underlay the chapel. Probes and soundings were undertaken to discover where this might be, but without success. Perhaps this is where the many theories of hidden spaces and lost treasures started.

Sir William died in 1484 leaving only the east end built, and just a single cross wall of the intended transept. His son Sir Oliver completed the vault, but otherwise it was left as it is to this day with no crossing, no tower, no transept and no trace of the intended nave. In 1523 his grandson, another Sir William, endowed land for the building of the college, but in 1571 the forces of the Reformation caused these to be confiscated. The chapel was described as 'a house and monument of idolatrie, and nor ane place appointit for teaching the word and ministratioun of ye sacraments'. By 1592, by the orders of the General Assembly, the altars had been demolished and worship ceased. Now disused, the chapel suffered further indignity when in 1688 a mob entered and smashed as many windows and statues as it could.

Minor repairs were put in hand in 1736, but the windows were still shuttered and the building disused. Dorothy Wordsworth recorded that 'as nothing is done to keep it together, it must, in the end, fall'.

More thorough repairs were undertaken in the nineteenth century, and in 1861 the 3rd Earl of Rosslyn agreed that, after an interval of nearly three centuries, Sunday worship should begin again. Services are conducted to this day by the Episcopalian church, though the building still belongs to the Earl of Rosslyn.

The 5th Earl initiated a classic decline of the family fortunes by gambling away in six years almost his entire inheritance – properties, estates, coal mines, steam yacht. The estate could no longer support a private chapel, especially one as elaborate as this.

Wartime economies in 1942 nearly caused the closure of Rosslyn, when the ruinous cost of fuel and of upkeep was weighed against the tiny congregation. A more serious threat in the 1950s was an overconfident treatment applied to the stonework. It was cleaned with ammonia and gallons of water, then sealed with an impervious silica slurry. This was a big mistake, because water was sealed in, not out. The only solution was to slowly dry it out by covering the whole building with a plastic roof for several years, and allowing the wind to blow through it. The £10 million that the restoration cost, plus another £3 million for a visitor centre, was justified and subsidised by the thousands of visitors drawn largely by its fictional fame. As the present Earl writes, by visiting Rosslyn, you are helping us to care for it.

CHAPTER 6

(RE)MOVED

In or about the year AD 336 the Empress Helena, mother of the first Christian emperor Constantine the Great and a great seeker of holy relics herself, discovered the humble house of Mary in the Holy Land. Here in Nazareth, Mary and Joseph had brought up the child Jesus. The Empress commissioned a church to be built over the little house. The remains of her great basilica can still be seen today underneath the 1960s basilica of the Annunciation, designed by Giovanni Muzio.

In 1291, however, the house itself was lifted up bodily by angels and transported to a hilltop in present-day Slovakia. Its travels were by no means over, for in 1294 it was carried further, to Italy and a wooded hilltop belonging to Laureta: hence the name, Loreto. And again a year later to the present hilltop, where the town of Loreto and domed basilica are situated. As time went by the Holy House, Santa Casa, reproduced itself in many places around the world, among them Walsingham in Norfolk and opposite the Černín Palace in Prague. Every time the house appeared it took on the same modest dimensions and the same single window and two doors, although it might be clothed in great splendour. To the modern evidence-based mind all this may seem pure hokum, but to the medieval mind the evidence worked the other way round: if the Santa Casa did its job, if the lame were healed and sight restored to the blind, if the unbelieving found faith, then obviously it was the real thing.

In our more humdrum times a church can still occasionally flit, disappearing from one place and reappearing in another. In the 1960s the entire town of Most in the Czech Republic (Brux in German; either way the name means bridge) was bulldozed in order to get at the brown coal that lay underneath it. A utilitarian replacement town was built nearby, but it was decided that the great church of the Assumption, an airy late medieval building with slender columns supporting a high crystalline vault, should be moved bodily to a new site. A surprising decision to be taken in Communist times by a state that officially considered religion to be nonsense. The job was done in 1975, not by angels unfortunately, but oh-so-slowly, cradled in steelwork, along multiple rail tracks. No miracle, but a remarkable feat of engineering.

Now all the coal and dirty stuff is gone. There is nothing to show for it but carbon dioxide, water and an apocalyptic hole, now slowly healing over with vegetation. The church looks surprisingly at home in its new surroundings, even its small reconstructed crypt under the east end. It is only when you see the massive concrete raft underneath that you can believe it has been moved at all.

ALSAGER TO HASSALL GREEN, CHESHIRE

St Philip at Hassall Green is the most eye-catching church in this book, and the most cheerful. Not because of its size or magnificence, quite the opposite in fact: it is painted a bright candy-floss pink, with turquoise doors and windows. Southbound travellers on the M6 might be cheered by a glimpse of it in the verdant Cheshire landscape below, as might boaters struggling up the many locks of Heartbreak Hill on the Trent & Mersey Canal.

St Philip's is a tin tabernacle – a prefabricated building of corrugated iron, lightly framed in wood and lined with tongue-and-groove matchboarding. Tin tabernacles came in all sizes and shapes. This one, supplied by Isaac Dixon & Co. of Liverpool, is rather more Gothic than most, with a little spire, slightly crooked, a porch, pointed windows and even a rose of sorts over the door. In its bright paint it makes a charming picture.

▼ **Below**: *Pink! The tin tabernacle at Hassall Green, formerly at Alsager.*

Tin tabernacles were a regular feature of the great church-building era of the nineteenth century, often used as temporary accommodation while a permanent building was put up. Some were even made for export. They could be surprisingly elaborate, with aisles and steeples, but it is the simpler ones that have survived. Given a regular coat of paint there is no reason why they should not last indefinitely, and the cosy wood-lined interior and modest size makes them practical, well-loved and readily adaptable.

All is not what it seems, however. St Philip's was founded at Hassall Green in 1898, so how can we explain the building's date mark of 1883? The explanation is that it started off life as St Mary Magdalene in the nearby town of Alsager. A stone church had been designed by Paley & Austin of Lancaster, but the money was hard to raise and a temporary expedient was needed – hence the tin tabernacle. In fact the stone church never was finished properly; the bell still hangs in a makeshift shelter on the west gable instead of in the splendid tower that was intended.

The stone church, although incomplete, was ready to be consecrated in 1897. Once it was brought into use the tin church was unbolted and dismantled, ready to be disposed of. A group of farmers from Hassall Green happened to be in town, saw what was happening and bought it for £150. Once the minimal foundations had been put in, the kit of parts could be bolted together again and the little church was ready for another lease of life.

So the church vanished from its old site in the town, flitted, changed its name and reappeared on a new site out in the country. The crinkly tin needed a new coat of paint, so why not pink? If pink, why not a nice sea-green for the doors and windows? Pink for the pulpit, too, set off by blue for the benches.

▼ *Below*: *Paley & Austin's stone church at Alsager replaced the tabernacle, although it is still unfinished.*

▶ **Opposite page**: *Ramsbottom. St Andrew's (Dundee) Presbyterian church with its eye-catching steeple.*

RAMSBOTTOM TO WHALLEY RANGE

Here is a strange tale.

The Lancashire town of Ramsbottom owes much of its nineteenth-century industrial prosperity to the Grant family, calico printers from Strathspey in Scotland. That explains the dour Scottish accent of several of the more prominent buildings in town. In 1832–4 William Grant built St Andrew's church for Presbyterian worship, Scottish-style. The design may have been made by William himself, or perhaps by his brother Charles. Its tower has distinctive overhanging sentry boxes to the top corners, like that of Linlithgow.

Early Lancashire industrialists such as the Grants were Nonconformists almost to a man, but their sons often became more 'respectable' than their parents and inclined towards the established Church. A generation later, in 1871, William's nephew, also called William, wrested control of St Andrew's and transferred it to the Church of England.

Naturally this triggered a split in the congregation. Those who clung to their Presbyterian beliefs walked out. They founded another church close by, and called it St Andrew's (Dundee) Presbyterian church. It was deliberately made more fancy and impressive than the old St Andrew's. Designed by the local architects James and Robert Garnet, the new St Andrew's had a most unusual and eye-catching steeple. The tall spire, halfway up, breaks into an open and transparent temple of Gothic columns and arches, before resuming its upward trajectory. It gave a striking effect even on the most gloomy Pennine day.

In the 1920s, when the rift between the two congregations had been at

least partially healed, the newer St Andrew's was no longer needed. So it was knocked down. That was not, however, the end of the tale.

In the inner Manchester suburb of Whalley Range, a district of big villas, schools and halls of residence, the Roman Catholic church of English Martyrs stood incomplete. It had been built in 1895–6 by F.H. Oldham, but the money had run out with only the base of the tower completed. Not an unfamiliar scenario.

The dimensions were found to match, so in 1927 the dismantled spire of the second St Andrew's was purchased, transported stone by stone, and reassembled on top of the existing tower base. Supervising the operation, a tricky one, was the architect E. Bower Norris, more usually occupied in building Catholic churches in pale brick of Byzantine influence. So the eye-catching spire of St Andrew's (Dundee) Presbyterian church has flitted from industrial Lancashire, to rise once more in suburban Whalley Range, glorifying a Catholic church. Whalley Range can also show a building that started off life as the Manchester Aquarium and is now St Bede's School, and a Training College for Primitive Methodists that is now a Muslim grammar school. Architecture is no respecter of preconceived boundaries.

SAVING ST TEILO'S

The old church of St Teilo stood deep in the marshes at a place called Llandeilo Tal-y-Bont. It was built on a bend of the River Llwchwr where it winds up to Pontarddulais, between Swansea and Llanelli. The best way to reach it was by coracle. Typically Welsh, it was a low, towerless, simple but strong building standing in a walled churchyard. 'A little desolate white church and a white-walled graveyard' was Edward Thomas's description. Both church and churchyard wall were kept whitewashed. The place, always difficult of access, is cut off even more now by a triangular railway junction and by the end of the M4 where it turns into the A40. A new St Teilo's had been built in 1850–51 in a more convenient place, and the old was seldom used.

The last service was held in 1970. After that it fell rapidly into disrepair, and by 1984 it was a sorry sight, overgrown and stripped of its roof and its furnishings. It seemed to have no future. However, as the rain ran down the interior walls, dissolving layers of limewash, traces of medieval wall paintings came into view. A rare survival. So it was decided to dismantle the church and rebuild it at the Museum of Welsh Life at St Fagan's.

What was left of the building had to be rescued quickly, before it deteriorated further. Everything was numbered and recorded, then taken down. By 1995 there was nothing left on site; the old St Teilo's had gone.

The parts were put into storage while the next stage was decided. The Museum of Wales had a tricky question on their hands. If the church was to be rebuilt, what point in its 700-year life should be recreated? Which particular past were we talking about? There was nothing inevitable in the decision, and different decisions have been made in different cases. When the country house of Uppark in Sussex burnt down in August 1989, for instance, the National Trust's

This page: *The lost church of St Teilo has flitted. Here it is, recreated at the Museum of Welsh Life.*

decision was to recreate everything exactly as it had been on the day before the fire. On the other hand, when Forest House in Chester was restored in 2008 everything genuinely old was carefully preserved, but there was no attempt to recreate what had been lost; the new work is unmistakably new. In a striking comparison, this was the treatment decided on by the German Federal Government and Norman Foster in the 1990s for the Reichstag in Berlin.

Here it was the wall paintings that determined the answer. St Teilo's was to be recreated as it might have been on the eve of the Reformation, using the old materials wherever possible and basing the rest on the evidence of this and other comparable buildings.

A good deal had to be made new. New nave and chancel roof trusses had to be made, based on the old pattern. Replacement slates for the roof and the flags for the floor had to be sourced and reclaimed from elsewhere. The windows, which had been enlarged in the eighteenth century, needed to be recreated in their original form, based on fragments found in the walls. The surviving wall paintings were fragmentary and could not be displayed on the rebuilt walls. Instead, new work has been created, based upon the surviving fragments of the old. Authentic pigments and techniques were used as far as possible; the result is astonishingly bright. The rood screen was long gone and is entirely new, elaborately carved and partly gilded, with a row of saints in the panelling. A dramatic Doom is painted

above it. The font, alone of the furnishings, is the original one.

St Teilo's opened as an exhibit at St Fagan's in 2007, and very successful it is, too. It looks and feels right, and is much visited. The church gleams white in its new setting, as it did in old pictures. The walls of the church are pleasingly battered, giving an impression of strength and permanence. Trees crowd close. By modern standards the church is surprisingly bare inside: no pews or chairs, no organ or drum kit, no hymn books or newsletter, no flower vases or collecting box. But it is bright and colourful. A good teaching aid, but to what extent is it the same church? For at least a decade there was no St Teilo's, just a pile of numbered stones. Its new position, by a track at the edge of a wood, is attractive but there is no historic reason for it to be there. And, of course, the graveyard is empty: no dead 'uns.

We may question whether it is possible for us in the twenty-first century to recreate work of the 1530s. Is St Teilo's at St Fagan's an ancient church that appears to have flitted, or a museum exhibit which happens to incorporate some old materials? The only logical answer is yes: both. The figures of the wall paintings look dwarfish, cartoon-like and very modern. Their colours are scientifically mixed, and look it. The striations and flaws in the window glass are not the result of imperfect technique; they have had to be made specially, at extra expense. We keep trying, but we have not yet achieved time travel.

LOMBARD STREET, CITY OF LONDON, AND CHERTSEY ROAD, TWICKENHAM

Even now, after the Great Fire and the Blitz, not to mention road widening and skyrocketing land values, the City of London seems to be full of churches. One of the unexpected pleasures of the Square Mile is to spot amongst the glass towers of the bankers a demure white Wren steeple and a tiny churchyard offering a little oasis of peace.

Today there are still thirty-nine in the City, most of them by Christopher Wren. But many have gone. Another ten churches are represented just by their towers, and twenty-one Wren churches have been lost altogether, including gems such as St Benet Fink and St Mildred Bread Street. St Mary Aldermanbury has emigrated to the United States, and can now be seen in Fulton, Missouri.

All Hallows Lombard Street, or most of it, has decamped to the suburbs, and now stands in a 1930s milieu on the Chertsey Bypass, close to Twickenham rugby ground.

The old All Hallows was nicknamed 'the church invisible'. Tucked away in the banking district of Lombard Street, it was entirely hidden behind surrounding buildings. A small archway, an iron gate, and a faded notice were the only external sign of its existence. If the gate was open, which wasn't often, a covered passageway led through to a little paved churchyard and the south door in the tower.

Wren's All Hallows was a plain building, undistinguished externally and simple in plan. It had replaced a church of ancient, indeed pre-Norman, foundation. Started in 1686 though not complete until 1694, it was his last City church because, although it was in the middle of the blaze, the old church and tower had

▼ **Below**: *All Hallows Lombard Street, as it was in the City of London.*

withstood better than most. Although plain outside, it was exceptionally rich in its furnishings, even for the City. Wealthy bankers made sure of that. The canopied pulpit and the magnificent reredos, probably by Grinling Gibbons, were particularly admired, but the whole ensemble typified the robust exuberance of London's seventeenth-century carvers. The hallowed interior was made even richer when other churches closed and furnishings were brought here.

All Hallows Lombard Street finally closed in 1937. There was considerable resistance to its demolition, not least from the City Corporation, but the site had been sold to Barclays Bank and it was taken down in 1938. There is no obvious sign of its existence on the old site today.

All was not lost. The suburbs were burgeoning, and a new church was needed in Twickenham. The building of Twickenham Bridge in 1931–3 (by Maxwell Ayrton with Alfred Dryland engineer) and the Chertsey Road had opened up a big new hinterland, soon to be built up with the typical 'Bayko' semis of the time. Here was a fine if plain Portland stone tower and a splendid and complete range of fittings ready for reuse. Given a spacious and prominent site, the architect Robert Atkinson was commissioned to build a new church to incorporate the old tower and to be furnished with the old fittings. Work started in 1939 and the new All Hallows opened in 1940.

Just in time. From September nightly air raids lit up the sky, and in a single concentrated attack at the end of December 1940 nineteen of the remaining City churches were lost, as recounted in chapter 9.

In its new setting All Hallows has changed its proportions. From the dual carriageway, the tower, virtually invisible in London, looks slim and unconscionably tall. In the City, even tall steeples such as St Bride Fleet Street are dwarfed by the high buildings all around. Wren had designed the tower to grow out of the building. Here it is almost detached, with just a low cloister to connect it with the church. It is balanced on the other side by the vicarage, enclosing a U-shaped courtyard.

It was an odd sort of job, to build a new church around existing fittings. So many dimensions were predetermined. Atkinson's church is quiet

in character, of brick with tall plain-glazed arched windows. His interior has columns and aisles, which gives it a strong longitudinal axis. Wren's church was a single space without columns, and so felt squarer, more centralised. The new church has a canted ceiling with a diagonal grid of ribs. Wren's was strongly coved at the edges but flat in the middle. The old City church was dark and brown, rich and dusty, like St Mary Abchurch today. All Hallows in Twickenham is bright and light, the dark wood of the furnishings contrasted with the clean white of the walls. It is interesting to see the side chapel, where Atkinson could be his own man: cool and white, with a gently elliptical plaster vault, carpeting and chairs.

We enter through Atkinson's 1930s west door, and then through Wren's wide dark oak screen with

◀ **Left**: *All Hallows at Twickenham. The complete fittings look reasonably at home in a new building.*

its cherub doorways. Straight ahead is the splendid altarpiece, so typical of London churches, with its many pediments. To one side is the magnificent pulpit with its oversized tester. At the back is the charming font and font cover, with more cherubs. The Renatus Harris organ of 1708 is in the gallery. There are many smaller items, too: bread cupboard, sword rests. It was a very thorough rescue, not just a token.

What reinforces the oddness of a flitted church is that all the commemorative monuments were transferred to the new building along with the furniture. Monuments to City mercers, bankers, doctors, admirals. Monuments with trumpeting angels, cherubs, weeping ladies, urns. But, of course, none of the bodies, so the customary phrases 'near this spot', 'beneath this monument' and even the ordinary 'here lies' mean nothing in their new setting. To complicate matters further, some of them have been moved once already, for instance the fine tablet to Thomas Lewis, 1704, which came from St Dionis Backchurch. Only time will tell whether an uprooted church can really take root again in a new place.

All Hallows in Twickenham seems proud of its unusual inheritance, but it is one remove from reality. The needs of a twentieth-century church and of a twenty-first-century suburban congregation are not the same as those of a mercantile class in seventeenth-century London. The reality shift was exemplified on a recent visit by hearing the church filled with the unbeatable organ music of Bach, only to discover that the sound was coming not from the Renatus Harris pipes but from a digital soundalike.

CHAPTER 7

LOST CATHEDRALS

~

In the year AD 313 the Emperor Constantine embraced Christianity, and the Christian Church, officially recognised at last, came out of hiding. The very next year the fledgling Church started to set up administrative territories on the Roman model. These were called dioceses and each was in the care of a bishop. Only the bishop can ordain priests and consecrate new churches.

The cathedral is the bishop's church. It contains the bishop's chair, the *cathedra*, which is its only defining feature. Everything else – towers, canons, choirs, closes – may be considered desirable to do the thing properly but can be dispensed with. So Beverley Minster, however magnificent, is not a cathedral, but St Asaph is, and a very venerable one at that.

A cathedral is sacred. It is built as worship as well as for worship. As a cathedral slowly rises and takes shape, so worship is taking place. In the recent reconstruction of the famous Frauenkirche in Dresden we have seen something like this, and perhaps too in the slow arising of La Sagrada Familia in Barcelona long after its architect's death. When the building is finally complete, or is stopped incomplete, then something falls out of the psyche of the community. However, cathedral building today does not always involve the community wholeheartedly. The mayor and corporation of Coventry in the 1950s were apparently hostile to the building of a new cathedral, and the populace of Liverpool in the 1960s may have been indifferent to the rising in their midst of two great twentieth-century cathedrals, one slowly and one quickly.

Part of the fascination of cathedrals is the way that they can survive disaster and rise again when all seems lost. The great cathedrals are, paradoxically, both hard to keep up and hard to knock down: fragile and immensely strong at the same time. This is because they take the properties of stone to its limit and even beyond. Mass is balanced against mass, thrusts are diverted down flying buttresses and sent on their way by heavy pinnacles. A Gothic cathedral is in a state of dynamic equilibrium not massive stasis.

On 19 April 1944 the great cathedral of Rouen was hit by four high-explosive bombs, one of which took out one of the four piers of the high crossing tower. Incredibly it stood, teetering upon three legs, until the amazingly brave workers underneath could shore it up. By contrast at lunchtime on Thursday 21 February 1861 the central tower and spire of Chichester Cathedral fell down all by itself, simply telescoping into the middle of the church in a cloud of dust.

THE VANISHING CATHEDRAL OF ELMHAM

On my Ordnance Survey Landranger map no. 132 for North West Norfolk, the track of one of Dr Beeching's axed railways heads north from the market town of Dereham. Passing the village of North Elmham it is intersected by the intriguing words 'Saxon Cathedral (remains of)'.

   Cathedrals are surprisingly peripatetic. The Bishopric of Lincoln started off in the Oxfordshire village of Dorchester-on-Thames. When the clergy of Old Sarum tired of the arid heights and the oppressive presence of its garrison they decamped to lower land and built a new cathedral and town, declaring, 'Let us descend joyfully to the plains, where the valley abounds in corn, where the fields are beautiful and where there is freedom from oppression'. The new Salisbury Cathedral, started in 1220, the same year as Amiens, was built rapidly to a single plan. As a result it is our purest and least quirky cathedral. Salisbury flourishes. Old Sarum is deserted; nothing there but wind and ruins and an English Heritage car park.

This page: A lost cathedral? Unexcavated ruins at Elmham.

The See for East Anglia was established by St Felix in the year 630 or 631 at a place called Dommoc. This was probably the port of Dunwich, near Southwold (see chapter 4). In 672 the bishopric was divided into two: Dunwich for what would become Suffolk, and Elmham for Norfolk. In the 950s the two were reunited at Elmham under Bishop Athulf, but in 1071 it moved to the then thriving metropolis of Thetford, before finally coming to rest at Norwich in 1094.

So Elmham only functioned as a cathedral for a relatively short time. But during that period, on Christmas Day 855, Bishop Humbert of Elmham crowned Edmund the Martyr King of the East Saxons at Chapel Barn, near Bures in Suffolk (see chapter 3).

Today there is nothing to be seen at Dunwich, and not much at Thetford either. 'The great days of Thetford are over,' says Nikolaus Pevsner. So what

of Elmham? The first problem is that there are two Elmhams, North and South. Strangely, both places show the remains of early churches. At South Elmham in Suffolk are the intriguing foundations of a Saxon minster with a wide apse and a broad west tower. North Elmham seems the most likely candidate, however – but do the ruins belong to the cathedral?

It is pretty spot, and the ruined church is an intriguing one. It stands in the bailey of a castle, overshadowed by the much higher motte – exactly the same situation as Old Sarum, though on a smaller scale. The high banks of the castle give a good overview.

The church was long and narrow. It had a massive Westwerk, or tower, which may have had an upper chapel reached by a turning stair. Then comes a long, thin nave, and then a cross transept with the apse opening straight off it, as St Paul's without the

Walls in Rome, although tiny in comparison. Two square chambers in the armpits of transept and nave were probably towers as well. The walls, which stand to considerable height, are built of an extraordinary puddingstone, like rough concrete. English Heritage suggest that it was probably painted all white; with its three towers it would have made an impressive sight.

Remembering again that this is very small in comparison, the ruin resembles one of Cologne's early churches such as St Pantaleon. A distinctive feature is the little quarter-round fillers in the angles of the transept towers. These could be a memory of the turrets that fill the corners of St Maria im Kapital or one of the other Cologne churches. They also occur in Norwich Cathedral. The uniting factor is that Bishop Herbert de Losinga, while maintaining a palace, estate and chapel at Elmham, founded Norwich Cathedral.

The ruin at Elmham is doubly confusing because in 1388 Bishop Despencer got permission to convert it into a semi-fortified manor, making twin towers to flank his front door and a hall in the upper part of the nave.

Is this the cathedral, though? The booklet of 1976 is firm, and so is the OS map: yes, it is. Its successor of 2007 is much more circumspect, calling it merely the site of a cathedral. The current thinking is that the church whose remains we have been examining was built around 1100, after the see had moved, to serve the bishop's country palace and estate. So Elmham Cathedral has disappeared once more into the mists of time. Whatever the truth, the bishop's defining seat or cathedra that is now at Norwich once stood here, at Elmham.

◀ **Left**: *The same site displayed, though still mysterious. View from the west, with Despencer's turreted doorway on the right.*

▲ **Above**: *Elmham. Puddingstone construction, originally plastered and whitewashed.*

ELGIN, THE LANTHORN OF THE NORTH

There are no cathedrals of medieval origin in Scotland. Scotland has had a stormy history, in every sense. The Scottish Church was reformed in 1560, when most of the cathedrals were deserted, and the office of bishop abolished altogether in 1689–90. It was left to the Catholic and Episcopalian churches to found new bishoprics and build new cathedrals; the Church of Scotland recognises no such office and therefore has no cathedrals.

The ancient cathedrals, which had been in decline for some time, were deserted and left to their fate. Most were unroofed, some largely demolished. Only Glasgow and Kirkwall survived more or less intact, though some of the others survived in part. A glance at any of the volumes of *The Buildings of Scotland* will show that the majority of old churches, like the cathedrals, are roofless ruins.

In the general destruction the most grievous loss is probably the great archepiscopal cathedral of St Andrews, of which so tantalisingly little is left, but we may legitimately regret the loss of the cathedral of Elgin, the Lanthorn of the North.

The early bishops of Moray were peripatetic, moving from Kineddar to Birnie and then Spynie. At

Spynie, between Elgin and the sea, was the bishop's palace. Standing on the banks of a sea loch, it is like a castle, with a mighty tower and attendant subsidiary towers within the curtain walls.

A permanent home and cathedral at Elgin was started in 1224. Like Salisbury a few years earlier, it was a new site. It was set out at the edge of town in a planned and spacious close called the chanonry. This, like the bishop's palace, was strongly defended; part of the strong perimeter wall survives, and one of the gates. Judging by the surviving precentor's house, a tower-like house with crowstepped gables and tiny windows, the canon's dwellings were strongly defensive in character as well. Within its close, however, the cathedral church itself was open, outward-looking and defenceless. 'The ornament of the realm', one of its bishops declared, 'the glory of the kingdom'.

The cathedral had three towers, the central one crowned with eight larger-than-life stone figures. One of them survives nearly complete, though now on the ground. A ring of chapels surrounded the nave, each one with a big traceried window. It looks as though each one was separately gabled. There was no triforium. Instead a long procession of lancets gave light from a tall clerestory. The south-east chapel that flanks the choir has retained its fine vaulting. On the other side, the polygonal chapterhouse also retains its vault.

The light of the Lanthorn of the North was dimmed in 1560 when the mass was abolished. The bishop and congregation simply moved out to the parish church. Lead from the roofs was stripped in 1568, the bells were melted down and the building fell into decay. Oddly enough, there was a Bishop of Moray long after the cathedral at Elgin had been deserted. As late as 1639 Bishop Guthrie, although barred by the Covenanters from preaching, was allowed to remain at Spynie. After his death in 1649 there was no bishop until 1662 when the office was revived under Charles II, and the last Bishop of Moray, though deprived of his office, did not die until 1707. Like the cathedral before it, the palace now fell into ruin, though it was still impressive. Even the sea loch dried up.

On Easter Day 1711 the central tower of the cathedral fell, taking most of the nave with it. The usual despoliation and stone-robbing was still taking place, but in 1807 a 'drouthy cobbler' called John Shanks was given the job of keeper or caretaker. In between showing visitors around, he worked tirelessly to clear the rubbish and rubble, perhaps removing much of archaeological value but nevertheless making the place presentable. Historic Scotland continue to make improvements, having recently reroofed the chapterhouse and the west towers.

Elgin Cathedral is a beauty, even in ruin. Its twin west towers, complete except for their tops, rise at the end of a walk through public gardens. Between them stretches a huge window, bearing just a few stubs of its ornamental tracery. The nave, missing its arcades and most of its outer walls, is open to the sky. The chancel is more complete, terminating in a fine show of windowing in two storeys of five lancets and a rose, between fat turrets.

Elgin is very lightly built compared with a Norman building like St Magnus at Kirkwall. St Magnus is all solid masonry and small windows; altogether massy, and almost claustrophobic inside. Elgin is structurally quite hollow, its walls opened up in French style. There was no high vault; instead it had an open wooden barrel ceiling, like Carlisle. A continuous passageway within the walls allowed one to walk right round the cross of the building at clerestory level. Another higher walkway wound right the way round the outside at parapet level, coming inside to cross behind the four end gables. Access to all these higher levels is thoroughly thought out. You can still climb up the south-west tower to the first level, enjoying the lovely little vault over this flight, then cross a bridge above the west door to the other tower. Turning stairs up either tower, climb to the next level and another bridge on the west windowsill, giving access to the clerestory walkway. Another level ascends for the parapet walkway and an external bridge over the top of the west window. Meanwhile, a turning stair next to the chapterhouse gives direct access over the north-west aisle gable to the turrets at the east end. There is evidently another turning stair in the north transept, presumably to get up to the vanished central tower.

When the rest of the church fell into ruin the octagonal chapterhouse alone was kept in reasonable repair by the town's incorporated trades, who used it as a meeting room. Inside, seating ranges round the walls and a beautiful vault fans out from a single central column. It is very lantern-like, even though the windows were made smaller and the tracery chunkier in the 1490s.

The cathedral's nickname, 'the Lanthorn of the North', was more than a figure of speech. In its northern context the cathedral, with its skeletal construction and great windows, was a marvel. It truly was a lantern, shining its light out into the gloom of the northern night, and its loss is all the more grievous.

PAUL'S

It was always familiarly called Paul's in Pepys's time, not the correct St Paul's Cathedral and certainly never London Cathedral.

The medieval cathedral of the City of London was in many respects the greatest in the land. It was the tallest, its spire reaching to a vertiginous 460 or even 500 feet, according to different estimates; in

either case considerably taller than Salisbury, which holds the present record. It was immensely long: at 586 feet it was a full double-twelver, i.e. twelve bays to the central crossing and another twelve after that. Lichfield, admittedly one of the smaller cathedrals, is for comparison a double-eighter measuring 370 feet. Paul's was so long that two parish churches came to be incorporated in the fabric, one at each end. The parish congregation of St Faith, the guild church of the Stationers Company, was accommodated in the spacious crypt which underlay the whole east end. It may have been the most beautiful, renowned for its stained glass, for the magnificent rose window at the east end, and for the open lantern tower. Its most distinctive feature was the flying stone props to the central tower, like stone scaffolding. Something similar can be seen at Gloucester Cathedral today, but these were fully detached, and unmistakable in any view.

We can see models and reconstructions of the building, but its life is harder to recapture. St Paul's was central to the life of the city. Deals and bargains of every kind were sealed and concluded

1629 called it 'the whole world's map, which you may here behold in its perfectest motion, jostling and turning ... a vast confusion of languages, and were the steeple not sanctified, nothing could be liker Babel'. The poet John Donne, intensely sensual yet deeply spiritual, was appointed dean in 1621 and was buried in the old cathedral in 1631. Public gatherings were held at Paul's Cross, which stood in the north-east area of the churchyard by Cheapside. Here, too, was a detached bell tower of the 1220s, with four bells and a spire. On the south side, sheltering in the angle between nave and transept, was the cloister, tightly but richly planned on two storeys. In the middle of that was the polygonal chapterhouse, also built on two storeys and richly appointed. The printers and binders, pamphleteers and booksellers of the book trade clustered in the surrounding alleys, using the

in the cavernous reaches ('Paul's walk') of the nave. The rather forlorn notice still to be seen in Wells Cathedral – 'It is requested by the Dean and Chapter that all persons forbear walking or talking in the aisles or nave of this cathedral during the time of Divine Service' – indicates that people do walk and talk during divine service. In Paul's, things went further: stalls were set up against the pillars – booksellers, seamstresses, tobacconists, and no doubt more shady businesses in the darker corners. Bishop Earle in

◀ **Opposite page**: *Sermon at Paul's cross.*

◀ **Left**: *Grafitti at Ashwell Church.*

▼ **Below**: *Wenceslaus Hollar's drawing of Old St Paul's.*

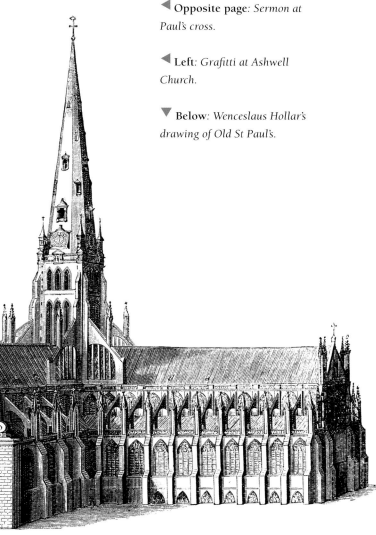

crypt chapel of St Faith as their guild church. St Paul's School, Dean Colet's great centre of the New Learning, stood next to the east end.

Old St Paul's, like all our cathedrals, suffered its share of catastrophe over the years. The spire, of wood and lead like that of Chesterfield (but not twisted), was struck by lightning in 1561. Dean Milman was there: 'Lightning was seen to flash into an aperture in the steeple. The fire burned downwards for four hours with irresistible force, the bells melted, the timber blazed, the stones crumbled and fell.' It was never replaced. In the 1630s, the great Inigo Jones transformed the west end, classicising the windows and adding a new portico in a magnificent, though unsympathetic, Roman style. But the work, indeed cathedral business of all kinds, came to an unceremonious halt on the outbreak of civil war in 1642.

After the Restoration, Charles II, with his architect Christopher Wren, gave some thought to further modernisation. Scaffolding was erected around the tower in readiness. A Royal Commission was established, and indeed on 27 August 1666 had agreed to start work. But within a week, all was lost.

In the early hours of 2 September Samuel Pepys was woken by his maid Jane who had seen a great fire from her window. Not thinking too much of it, Pepys went back to bed, but in the morning he walked to the Tower 'and there got up upon one of the high places, Sir J. Robinsons little son going up with me; and there I did see the houses at that end of the bridge all on fire, and an infinite great fire on this and the other side the end of the bridge ... So down, with my heart full of trouble, to the Lieutenant of the Tower, who tells me that it began this morning in the King's bakers house in Pudding lane, and that it hath burned down St. Magnes Church and most of Fishstreete already.'

From the river Pepys saw the 'fire as only one entire arch of fire from this to the other side of the bridge, and in a bow up the hill, for an arch of above a mile long. It made me weep to see it. The churches, houses, and all on fire and flaming at once, and a horrid noise the flames made, and the cracking of houses at their ruine.'

The burnt-out cathedral under demolition c. 1672. Thomas Wyck drew the scene from the north east, showing the south transept largely complete.

By Tuesday the 3rd the fire had reached the cathedral. The houses which were clustered around burst into flames with the intense heat. The wooden scaffolding around the tower kindled, enveloping the whole upper part of the fabric in a network of fire. Silvery streams of molten lead cascaded 'sparkling, flashing, hissing, and consuming all before it' down the walls. Finally, so intense was the heat that it set fire to the thousands of books hastily stacked for safety in St Faith's crypt. 'The stones of St Paul's flew like grenades, the melting lead running down the streets in a stream, and the very pavements glowing with fiery redness,' wrote John Evelyn. On the 7th

proved that it couldn't be done, the order was given to demolish the lot – with considerable difficulty, such was the strength of the old building even now – and start again. Over the next half-century Wren's classical cathedral arose in its place. Christopher Wren's building, muscular in its proportions, is neither as long nor as tall as the medieval cathedral. It is curious that the old familiar name Paul's didn't transfer to the new St Paul's Cathedral, any more than the old tuppence and thruppence transferred to our decimal coinage in 1971.

Almost nothing of the old Paul's is left, but that hasn't stopped scholars and historians from sifting the evidence and mentally recreating it. The footprint of part of the cloister and chapterhouse is marked outside the present building, showing that the alignment of old and new is not quite the same. Medieval drawings of buildings are rare, but contemporary images of the old cathedral can be found in some unlikely places. The parish church of Ashwell in Hertfordshire is lined on the inside with soft white stone that lends itself to being defaced. Among several specimens of medieval graffiti is a surprisingly accurate and detailed architectural drawing of a great church. Incised probably in the late fifteenth century, this is undoubtedly St Paul's, with its unmistakable flyers propping the tower, its eastern rose window and even its detached belfry. There is a possible connection in that the famous master mason John Wastell (1460–1515) came from Ashwell. His best-known work is Bell Harry, the central tower of Canterbury Cathedral.

Most of our knowledge of old St Paul's comes from a set of forty-four engravings by Wenceslaus Hollar (1607–77) which were published in 1657. Born in Prague, he came to London with the Earl of Arundel in 1637. From these have been spun off the Victorian reconstructions of Benjamin Ferrey and modern imaginings of the lost building, but in truth we know more about the unbuilt early stages of Christopher Wren's Baroque cathedral than we do about its mighty predecessor that dominated London for so long.

Pepys went 'by water to Paul's wharfe. Walked thence and saw all the town burned, and a miserable sight of Pauls church, with all the roofs fallen and the body of the Quire fallen into St Fayths – Paul's school also – Ludgate – Fleet Street – my father's house, and a good part of the Temple the like.'

A little monument, the Golden Boy of Pye Corner in Smithfield, marks where the fire finally stopped. Most of the city was in ruins, but among the ashes the calcined bones of the cathedral, solidly built of stone, were still standing. The first thought was to contrive a new cathedral around the columns and walls that refused to fall, but after a couple of accidents had

LLANDAFF: THE LOST TEMPLE

Llandaff, on the outskirts of Cardiff, is an ancient foundation, tracing its origins to St Teilo in around AD 546. We can imagine it as a small monastic settlement hidden from marauders in the steep Taff valley. In the 1120s Bishop Urban replaced it with a grander building in the Norman style; his splendid chancel arch survives. Over the centuries it has had an extraordinarily chequered history, with more than its share of misfortune but also some lucky choices. Today the cathedral of Llandaff is anything but lost, unless you count the peculiar way its non-identical twin steeples seem to emerge from a hole in the ground. On the contrary, it is a particularly pleasing place, highly individual, atmospheric and full of interest.

Llandaff has never been rich, and after the Reformation it fell on particularly hard times. Bishop Blethin in 1584 described it as '*derelicta, solatioque*

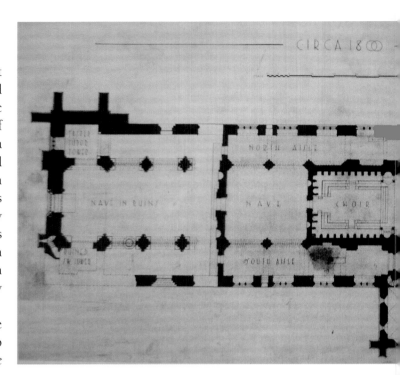

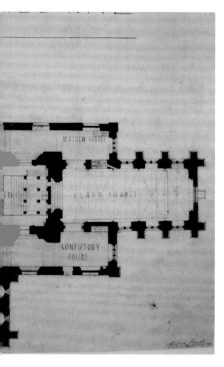

▼ **Below**: *Llandaff. Victorian restoration has expunged all memory of the Italian Temple.*

▼ **Below left**: *The Gothic west front is abandoned; Wood's Temple with its corner urns can be glimpsed behind.*

◀ **Left**: *A plan of c.1800 shows John Wood's Italian Temple squatting in the ruinous cathedral.*

pastorali destituta' – derelict and destitute of pastoral care. The cathedral church was untidy, full of dirt and almost beyond repair. By 1692 the roof was unsafe. In 1703 pinnacles fell and in 1722 the south tower collapsed altogether, destroying much of the nave. Only the eastern parts were now usable. The choristers and organists were dismissed. Bishops, poorly remunerated, were absentees and unashamedly pluralist. The most notorious was Richard Watson, Bishop of Llandaff, 1782–1816. 'Most vain and self-approving,' says Joseph Farington (diary, 26 October 1808), the 'extreme of egotists'. He made his home far away in Windermere, having first managed to procure the chair of Chemistry at Cambridge despite, on his own admission, knowing nothing about the subject. He was a quick learner. In 1771 he managed to secure the Regius Chair of Divinity, having by 'hard travelling and adroitness' got himself a doctorate the day before the election.

The cathedral at Llandaff that Bishop Watson so conspicuously neglected was a very strange affair. In 1734 Bishop John Harris, in despair over the condition of the fabric, had commissioned John Wood of Bath to rig up something usable within the Gothic ruins. Unexpectedly Wood, the architect of Queen Square, The Circus and much else in Georgian Bath, seems to have relished the job. Wood's character was very much at odds with the apparent rationality of his squares and crescents. An enthusiastic antiquary, he was full of half-baked notions concerning early Britons, druids and the lost Temple of Jerusalem. He picked up Browne Willis's theory of 1718 that the first church at Llandaff had been built in Roman times, and was proportioned to accord with Solomon's Temple. So he tried to recreate something like it.

The biblical account in the first book of Kings, chapter six, describes the temple as a building proportioned 60 long: 20 wide: 30, its plan divided into three squares. Wood managed to wangle this out of the six central bays of the cathedral. The outer rooms described in Kings were supplied by the aisles, and the courts of the temple by the roofless western bays of the Gothic church. The approach must have been extraordinary. Instead of ascending to the glorious Temple on the mountain top, you

Llandaff Cathedral, Choir East

had to wind steeply down the path from Cathedral Green to a mossy ruin. Facing you was the ivy-clad stump of the south-west tower and the crumbling walls of the nave. At the bottom of the path the door and windows of the Gothic west front gaped emptily. The north-west tower was still sound, but shorn of its crown of pinnacles. Through the old west door was a sight to gladden the heart of any eighteenth-century Romantic: the arches of the Gothic nave stood verdant and open to the sky. Grass and young trees flourished on the wall tops. Facing you was the pedimented front of Wood's temple, elegantly proportioned, with a Venetian window above the pedimented doorway. Pushing open this second entrance you entered a cool white interior of classical harmony, lit by clear glass in round-topped windows and crowned by a high plaster vault. The altar stood where it stands now, but under a Corinthian baldacchino with eight columns and a pediment – a miniature temple within the temple. Smaller temple-ettes to right and left served as pulpit and reading desk. Bishop Urban's chancel arch behind the altar had been walled in, as had the choir, but the two remaining bays of the nave were allowed to flow into the aisles which surrounded the whole. Had John Wood the antiquary read of the Duomo of Syracuse in Sicily, where the Greek temple

of Athena of c. 480 BC is fossilised within the present cathedral? In a back-to-front kind of way his temple at Llandaff did the same thing.

The classical temple sheltering within a crumbling Gothic ruin must have made a highly picturesque sight to eighteenth-century eyes. By the nineteenth century, however, the whole thing was anathema. The theories of A.W.N. Pugin had utterly demolished the idea of a classical temple for Christian worship, trumpeting Gothic as the only true style. And so Wood's temple was taken down, and the Gothic cathedral repaired, rebuilt where necessary, and made good. Llandaff's fortunes were looking up with the industrialisation of Cardiff. This time Llandaff was lucky in its chosen architect, for the young John Pritchard, son of one of the Vicars Choral, was a man of rare talent. His new south-west tower and spire are exceptionally good, both soaring and securely based. Its mismatch with the old north-west tower is, counter-intuitively, entirely successful, as is proved also at Chartres and Antwerp. Pritchard worked in partnership with John Pollard Seddon, an initiate of the Pre-Raphaelites, which explains the Rossetti altarpiece and the surviving Morris windows.

John Wood's temple at Llandaff is utterly lost. It is hard to find any evidence today that it ever

◀ **Left**: *Disaster strikes Llandaff again in 1941.*

▶ **Opposite page**: *George Pace's post-war restoration of the cathedral; a memorable amalgam of old and new.*

existed. Most accounts of the cathedral's history draw a discreet veil over it, as though it were a shameful episode to be forgotten as soon as possible. And yet, as Newman writes in *The Buildings of Wales – Glamorgan,* it was a much more serious piece of architecture than later critics imagined.

Llandaff's troubles were not over. On 2 January 1941 the cathedral was nearly lost all over again when it was hit by a German landmine. Its parachute cables snagged on Pritchard's south-west spire, dislodging its top 15 feet, and then it exploded immediately outside the south aisle. The spot is marked today by an upright slate and a circle delineating the crater.

The roofs were destroyed, all the windows blown out, the walls shaken and much of the interior wrecked. The dean, David Jones, was in the cathedral at the time, and never fully recovered from his injuries.

After an emergency patch-up the eastern parts of the building were back in use by April 1942, but the rest had to wait. In 1948 the deaths of both the dean and the cathedral architect, Sir Charles Nicholson, led to the appointment of a young and relatively untried architect, George Pace of York, to complete the repairs and bring the building into the twentieth century.

Pace was a modernist, and his work was not always successful. Here, however, he achieved a happy fusion of the old and boldly new. His boldest stroke was the concrete parabolic arch, which stands in place of the traditional rood screen, or pulpitum, carrying a section of the organ in an oval case and fronted by an Epstein sculpture of Christ in Majesty.

This to my mind is extremely successful. You step down into Llandaff Cathedral. Down the steep hill and then down again through the west doors. Epstein's *Majestas* is at eye level as you enter, as Pritchard's spire had been on the outside descent. Although Llandaff is small by the standards of English or French cathedrals, its interior is satisfyingly complex, revolving around the Pace pulpitum and then punctuated by the splendid Norman arch of Bishop Urban. This is Llandaff's unique signature.

UNCOMPLETED BUSINESS: THE EPISCOPAL CATHEDRAL OF ST JOHN THE DIVINE, OBAN

Many cathedrals show signs of unfinished business. The money may have run out, the ground may have proved unsuitable, or the will that has driven the project along may simply be exhausted. Some never got started, like R.C. Carpenter's 1850s design for a new Manchester Cathedral, or Taizé in Burgundy, which continues to operate from tents and shacks. Lutyens' vast domed Liverpool Catholic Cathedral never got further than half of the crypt, although even that is a mighty work. Towers and west fronts are especially liable to remain unachieved, since they are built last and are non-essential. Chartres Cathedral should have seven towers, Rheims nine. Chester should have a mighty south-west tower. Sometimes it looks as though the masons were simply sent home one lunchtime and never returned, as at Dordrecht in Holland where they left the jagged tower top to be disguised with four comical clocks.

Here in Oban is a cathedral that has never really come to fruition, in spite of repeated efforts. It is a mishmash of half-finished designs and frustrated ambition, executed in two colours of stone, designed in two different styles, oriented in two different directions, propped up with steel, and covered with a worrying overcomplication of roofs. The site is a good one but too small, too hemmed in for an ambitious building. The problems are all too obvious round the back – an alleyscape of bins, parked cars, blocked arches, unfinished windows, and an empty scoop for an intended spiral stair.

First, a potted history. The Diocese of Argyll and the Isles was revived by the Episcopalians in 1846. In 1864 a modest church was built here in George Street. It was designed in simple lancet style in the local greenish stone, oriented east–west. The chancel faced inland and was built right up to the street frontage, and a path led to the entrance at the

▲ **Above**: *The original church of 1864 and 1881 was relegated to a narthex when the axis was changed.*

◀ **Opposite**: *Oban Episcopal Cathedral. The street frontage.*

back, towards the harbour.

In 1881 grand plans were prepared by Ross & Mackintosh for a proper cathedral with central tower, but they came to naught. Instead, a modest aisle was added on the south side, allowing for a porch direct to the street, which had now become the principal thoroughfare of the town. A small tower next to the porch was proposed but not built. So now we had an enlarged but still modest church, with two parallel roofs.

In 1908 more grand plans were prepared, this time by James Chalmers (1858–1927), architect and lay preacher of Glasgow. He proposed turning the axis through 90 degrees so that the chancel would be to the north. The 1864 nave would be incorporated crossways into the new one, and the 1881 aisle become a narthex. This expedient has been tried in several places but it never works: see examples from Sheffield to Siena. Construction started in grand style but was abandoned in 1910, with a chancel built on the new axis, the crossing space but no tower, one transept and not the other, and one bay of the nave. They were built of red St Bees stone, which made an unhappy contrast with the greenish stone of the old work. Inside, the unfinished arcade had to be propped with massive raking steel shores, riveted battleship-style and painted grey. A strong visual demonstration of the thrust was generated by a row of arches.

More schemes were prepared in 1928, but once again nothing came of them. Work began again in 1958–68. Once more a whole new design was made, but frustrated. What was done was that the 1864 nave floor was raised to the same level as the 1908 work, but not the narthex (1881 aisle), so a flight of steps had to be made between the two. The original 1864 church had already lost its north wall and the northern half of its roof. Now the arcade between the 1864 nave and its old aisle was removed as well, to be replaced by a steel beam and a wall of glass, with sliding glass doors. It is an uncomfortable and very 1960s effect, for the valley and the two roofs appear to be resting only on glass.

More work was undertaken in 1987. Now the remaining south half of the 1864 nave roof was replaced by glass. So there is really very little left of the original church: just two end walls and half a roof. The green stone was painted red in an attempt to blend it with the newer work. More glazing was introduced over the Chalmers crossing, and structural worries necessitated the introduction of extra steelwork at high level, this time welded and painted red.

So there we are – so far. Confused?

Unlike the Roman Catholic cathedral on Oban's seafront, which is a finished statement (Giles Gilbert Scott, 1932 etc. and 'decidedly permanent'), the Episcopal cathedral is in a visible state of flux. A work in progress. The tensions and stresses set up by unrealisable ambition are there for all to see. It is a salutary lesson. If a cathedral is meant to be a sermon in stone, here we have one, and a memorable one at that.

▶ **Right**: *Oban Episcopal Cathedral, never fully achieved, visibly under stress, provides a sermon in itself.*

CHAPTER 8

CHAPELS

~

THE WAYSIDE CHAPEL

November 2006. A blowy late autumn day high in the North Pennines of Alston Moor, near Garrigill. The rank grass ripples, lapwings call and wheel, wide horizons beckon. A rare window of late sun picks out a big beech tree still magnificent in its autumn finery. Beneath it, in a little walled enclosure, is a lonely chapel. The chapel gate opens straight on to the moor.

      Redwing chapel (Congregational) was built in 1756, closed in 1977. The stone roof is thick with moss, the windows cloudy with damp. The simple furnishings have faded to a silvery grey, the walls to palest blue. In such a remote spot there is something almost luxurious about its gentle decay, but one wild Pennine night the roof will fall and that will be the end of the story.

The simpler and humbler chapels are often built in incidental places; by the wayside, at a crossroads, in a side street – wherever a sliver of land could be bought for not too much money. As time goes by the chapel might remain isolated, becoming an unregarded part of the landscape, but sometimes a settlement will gather round it so that the street or lane or even the whole community might take its name from the chapel. Names are the longest-lived of things, so a Chapel Lane or Tabor Street, or a town called Bethesda or Salem, might remember something that has long gone.

This page: Walker Barn, near Macclesfield.

During the Commonwealth (1649–60) not only was kingship abolished but the hierarchical structure of the English Church was largely done away with. Bishops were sacked, cathedrals redundant. After the Restoration in 1660 Charles II and parliament endeavoured to re-establish the Church with the Act of Uniformity of 1662. Bishops and cathedrals were reinstated, and the Book of Common Prayer introduced in an effort to standardise a particular form of worship. Its use was compulsory. It inspired furious debate and the first serious breakaways, such as the Quakers. More than 2,000 clergy of puritanical sympathies refused to conform, and were ejected from their livings. A further Act in 1664 made it illegal to hold alternative religious meetings of more than five

people, and the Five Mile Act banned ejected clergy from ministering in their old parishes. Nevertheless, dissenting congregations managed to gather out of doors, in each others' houses or in out-of-the-way meeting houses.

In the reign of William and Mary attitudes softened somewhat and in 1689 the Act of Toleration allowed freedom of worship – and chapel building. As an example, three chapels were built immediately in east Cheshire, one in Macclesfield, one in Knutsford and the third near Wilmslow. Their congregations were still uncertain of their freedom from persecution, so the Macclesfield (1689) one is hidden down a ginnel, the Wilmslow one (1693) out in the fields.

The essential distinguishing feature of a dissenting chapel is that it is autonomous under God, recognising no centralised human authority. The chapel belongs to its congregation. There is no particular obligation towards non-members, so it is very unusual to find a chapel unlocked outside service time. A chapel is not consecrated, nor is the building of it considered to be an act of worship. It is a building in which meetings for worship can conveniently take place. So there is no need for extensive heart-searching if circumstances make it no longer convenient. Chapels rarely have a tower or a clock – these are public things. Nevertheless, they generally make a show to the world at large, and are immediately recognisable for what they are. Early chapels such as the

▲ **Above**: *Redwing Chapel, Alston Moor.*

▲ **Above right**: *Abandoned and almost invisible: Wesleyan Chapel near Castle Frome, Herefordshire.*

three Macclesfield ones are quite domestic looking, but soon the type settled down to presenting a show front towards the street, symmetrical and usually classical in inspiration, plain longer sides with clear windows, and perhaps an extension at the back for the dais, organ and ancillary rooms. Bigger chapels will generally have two storeys, indicating the galleries within. The interior will be plain and unmysterious, well lit from clear windows, designed so that everyone can see and hear clearly. The blocks of pews will be focused on the pulpit, which stands for the exposition of the Word. In the corner might be a wheezy harmonium, on the wall perhaps a slow-ticking clock.

The trouble with dissent is that it tends to lead to more dissent. You could even argue that Henry VIII's breakaway from Rome engendered all the subsequent breakaways. Chapel congregations disagree, fragment and found other chapels. Often

there is a competitive element, so the new chapels may be unnecessarily big and grand.

Recent years have seen the opposite trend. As congregations shrink, so they amalgamate. The distinction between Wesleyan, Primitive and New Connexion Methodists no longer exists, and the United Reformed Church brought together Congregational and Presbyterian congregations. Further, different congregations may agree to use the same building. In Llandudno, for example, all the four Nonconformist congregations have agreed to worship in Seilo chapel of 1901–5, although how long this very grand building can be maintained even by four congregations remains to be seen.

Chapels are important in the lives of individuals and communities, but because they are fiercely independent they are hard to bring into any sort of survey or general study. Only when they were rapidly disappearing did the world at large wake up

to their unique importance. The SAVE document of 1980 which drew attention to the plight of the magnificent chapels of Yorkshire and the Pennines was a wake-up call, but already too late for some. It was only when three-quarters of the chapels of Cornwall had been lost that a proper survey of them was set in motion, and the same will be true of Wales.

　　When a chapel building closes it may be demolished, but they are adaptable buildings, especially the smaller ones, and can often find a new use: home, studio, showroom, restaurant, hostel, concert hall, library, museum, shop, even an exhibition of its former self. The building may be saved but the interior features are all liable to be lost in the process. These things can be preserved, too, although that will severely limit the new use of the building, but what cannot be artificially prolonged is the life that went with it all. Once it is gone it is gone. The fiery oratory and impassioned delivery of the preacher – what the Welsh call *hwyl*; the exhilarating and uplifting sound of a whole chapel in full voice; the sense of belonging, of being part of a close social group that would support you in joy or sorrow – though it could also ostracise you and cast you out, as George Eliot's Silas Marner found out.

▲ **Above**: *Primitive Methodist chapel, dated 1863, at Melverley.*

IN TOWN: EARLY CHAPELS IN FROME

In the wool towns of Somerset the Act of Toleration of 1689 coincided with a time of great industrial prosperity and religious ferment. The town of Frome was growing prodigiously, and a whole new industrial suburb was built in the Trinity area. When John Wesley visited he saw that the town was a hotbed of religious opinion, 'Anabaptists, Quakers, Presbyterians, Arians, Antinonians, Moravians and what not'. Dissenters of one sort or another greatly outnumbered Anglicans, not just among the millworkers but equally among the masters whose grander houses are so intimately juxtaposed with the weavers' cottages in this most intricate town.

In the pioneering days that followed the Act of Toleration, when there was not yet an accepted type of chapel architecture, three ambitious chapels within a stone's throw of one another were built by rival congregations.

Rook Lane chapel was the first and the grandest. It is prominently dated 1707. Its congregation, a direct breakaway from the parish church, followed their

This page: *Magnificent, but abandoned, chapel architecture at Rook Lane, Frome. The derelict chapel was restored in the 1990s.*

◀ **Left**: *Rook Lane chapel, side elevation.*

▼ **Below**: *Rook Lane. The original gallery and all the furnishings were lost; only the two giant stone columns remain.*

▶ **Opposite page**: *Almost invisible: Catherine Street Chapel, Frome.*

minister John Humfry when he was ejected from his living at St John's church. It was a self-governing and Congregational body, eventually being affiliated to the United Reformed Church. The chapel was built for Humfry by the wealthy clothier Robert Smith, who gave the land. Its builder and probable designer was James Pope. It is an astonishingly confident building, making a grand statement with its front of Bath stone, fully seven bays wide with a pediment and pedimented doorway. One of the first chapels in the country to issue such a challenge, it originally faced on to the narrow thoroughfare of Rook Lane. The creation of Bath Street in 1810 gave it much greater prominence, with a long sloping forecourt. Not so grand at the sides and back, though.

The inside was structured around two great Doric columns of stone, which supported the valley of the roof. Until the canals and railways allowed the importation of Scandinavian or American timbers, roof spans were limited by the size of English oak, so a system of internal supports was still essential.

The chapel was a major force in the town. In 1717 it was said that a congregation of 1,000 attendees was expected on a Sunday. However, its fortunes went into decline with several changes of minister, and in 1773 a section of the congregation broke away to build the new Zion chapel down the hill. When falling numbers in the twentieth century caused the congregations to merge again, the choice fell on Zion, and Rook Lane was redundant. In 2014 Zion was also due to close.

Rook Lane chapel closed in 1968, and was left empty and at risk for twenty-five years. A disused building is always vulnerable, and the chapel suffered much deterioration and damage. Internal fittings were removed or vandalised; even the wall monuments were destroyed. There were several efforts to rescue it; indeed, £63,000 was spent in the 1990s by the Somerset Buildings Trust on restoration work, but it was not until 2001 that it found the essential new use which guaranteed its future. An architectural practice employing twenty or so people made the building its headquarters. Their offices in the rebuilt gallery provide daily use, care and income, while an exhibition space and occasional evening

events, including a Frome architecture club, use the ground floor. An extension of 2002–3 at the back by the resident architects NVB (Nugent Vallis Brierley) provides the essential kitchens and toilets.

So Rook Lane, the most prominent building in town, was pulled back from the brink and its future now seems good.

Sheppards Barton/South Parade Baptist chapel was built just a year after Rook Lane, in 1708, though the congregation had already been meeting in the house of John Sheppard, a wool mill owner. It was Sheppard who gave the land. It followed the same plan and structural system as Rook Lane, and may have had the same designer. Although not quite as big, it was said to be better than Rook Lane because it was 'beautiful on all four sides'. This refers to the fact that Rook Lane was all front: a criticism

THE *South west* VIEW OF Mr KINGDONS MEETING HOUSE.

levelled at most chapels, then and now. However, when Sheppards Barton chapel was rebuilt in 1849 by J. Davis, presumably to eliminate the troublesome valley gutter, it was given a grand front and not much else. The front faced South Parade, hence the change of name. The chapel closed in the 1990s and is currently empty and to let, in a poor state. The schoolroom at the back, added in 1852, is now flats.

Badcox Lane/Catherine Street chapel was built in 1711 for a rival Baptist congregation. This was built to the same plan again – these three are a definite family – with two giant columns supporting the central valley. However, it was trapezoidal in outline because of its constricted site. A drawing made before 1806 by Stephen Whiting, with a small plan attached, shows a two-storey building with the door in the side and two tiers of plain two-light windows – much like a mill of the period. He must

◀ **Left**: *Early drawing of Catherine Street Chapel, as it was first built.*

▼ **Below**: *Although nearly invisible from Catherine Street, neighbouring gardens have a good view of the chapel.*

▶ **Right**: *The disused chapel interior, ready for disposal.*

have had trouble drawing it because it was built in the backlands, and has almost no street frontage; indeed, like the Saxon chapel at Bradford on Avon, or All Hallows on London's Lombard Street, it was virtually invisible. The chapel was also rebuilt in 1813, taller than before, though still invisible. It at last acquired a street presence only in 1845 when a Doric portico was built facing Catherine Street, hence the alternative name. Bizarrely, however, this could not be attached to the chapel itself, which was still hugged by buildings on every side, but opened into an internal backyard.

Catherine Street chapel closed in 1962 and was sold to Frome Urban District Council. It served as a public library for a spell, from 1964 to 1967. When a purpose-built library was erected by the river (now a toyshop) the chapel was slated for demolition, along with the neighbouring Temperance Hall, in order to provide a small car park. Reprieved, however, it was used as a furniture showroom for a spell. It is now divided into flats. And still invisible.

Lost as chapels, in a resurgent town like Frome all three have survived as buildings, but not before passing though a painful hiatus of uncertainty.

SALEM, EBENEZER, BETHESDA

Bethesda, Zion or Seion, Elim, Tabor, Salem, Ebenezer, Moriah, Horeb. The name, customarily displayed in the front gable, presupposes an intimate knowledge of the scriptures. Presbyterian, Congregational, Unitarian, Methodist, Independent, Primitive Methodist, New Connexion, Baptist, Pentecostal, Swedenborgian, Christadelphian: the denomination reflects endless dissent among dissenters. They may be grand town chapels with a show front to the street, an elaborate dais, ranks of organ pipes and tier upon tier of pews. Or a humble country chapel with its unassuming architecture and simple furnishings.

Salem: the name signifies the Holy City, the New Jerusalem: whole, safe and at peace. There are many Salems, including the American city famous for its 1692 witchcraft trials. This particular Salem is a rural Baptist chapel of 1850 at Cefncymerau, outside Llanbedr, near Harlech. More especially, it is a painting of that chapel made by Sidney Curnow Vosper in 1908. The painting has made the chapel famous, though its members are few.

Ten o'clock service is about to begin in the quiet chapel. An old lady with wizened face and pursed lips, clutching her Bible, makes her way to her pew. She wears a black steeple hat over her ruched bonnet. The clock shows that she is in time for the service, but just too late for the customary silence that precedes it. The other chapelgoers are already sitting quietly in their pews. It is

◀ **Left**: *Sidney Curnow Vosper's famous painting* Salem, *1908.*

▶ **Opposite page**: *Bethesda chapel gave its name to the town of Bethesda, Caernarvonshir – but is now closed.*

picture again in 1937, and it featured as a calendar for several years in the 1950s. So *Salem* entered the Welsh consciousness, standing for national identity in much the same way as Constable's *The Haywain* does in England or Raeburn's *The Skating Minister* in Scotland.

Vosper took a great deal of trouble over the picture, making many preliminary sketches with local people as models. The central figure was an elderly local lady, Sian Owen, though he had to use a wooden lay figure to get the folds of the shawl right.

A genre picture like this can compress a whole narrative in a single moment of captured time, but in *Salem* that narrative takes on two entirely different aspects. On the one hand we see a reassuring yet nostalgic narrative of Welsh identity, but on the other many people, especially children, have confessed to finding the picture frightening. There is certainly something deeply claustrophobic in the scene; it is easy to imagine the indrawn breath and tuts of disapproval that would have greeted Sian's late arrival and her showy costume, and the malicious gossip that would have circulated afterwards. Mind you, her pinched face and pursed lips suggest that she could give as good as she got.

easy to imagine the rustle of her black dress and the shuffling of her feet in the silence, and the sideways glances cast at her beautifully fringed Paisley shawl. Despite her downcast, rheumy eyes she commands all attention.

Vosper has somehow captured in this single image an entire essence. Here is old Wales, the rural Wales we would all like to remember, in a lost time untroubled by the travails of industry or of war. A time of simple communal faith where a small vanity could make a whole narrative.

The picture was bought from exhibition by William Lever – Lord Leverhulme – for 100 guineas, and now hangs in the Lady Lever Gallery at Port Sunlight in the Wirral. Lever had a good eye. He was a great believer in the power of art and its influence on ordinary people should they see it, and liked to hang original paintings in his canteens and social clubs. Nor was he one to miss a commercial opportunity. He offered free colour reproductions of *Salem* in return for Sunlight soap wrappers. It was hugely popular, and the reproductions hung in kitchens and parlours all over Wales. The Welsh League of Youth issued the

The words of Dylan Thomas's *Under Milk Wood* come to mind:

Listen. It is night in the chill, squat chapel,
hymning in
bonnet and brooch and bombazine black,
butterfly choker and bootlace bow, coughing
like nannygoats, sucking mintoes, fortywinking
hallelujah …

Some have seen more sinister things: a little face peering in at the window; and, worse, a grotesque devilish face with hooded eyes and long beard in the folds and fringe of her shawl. Vosper protested that he had intended no such thing, but that doesn't mean to say it isn't there. Once you have identified it, it is hard not to see it. But even setting that aside, is it possible to see in this one painting both the great strength of chapel life and the seeds of its ultimate decline?

The name, Ebenezer, often applied to chapels, means stone of help; the Rock of Ages. It was the place of battle between Israelites and Philistines.

A fingerpost off the A391 in west Cornwall indicates a place called Ebenezer in half a mile, and then the wonderfully named Luxulyan, birthplace of the equally wonderfully named architect Silvanus Trevail.

Many Cornish places are named after their own Celtic saint – Altarnun, Constantine, St Breock, St Ewe, St Kew, St Ives, and so on. This one is named after its chapel. But it is not much of place.

By the eighteenth century the Church of England in Cornwall was weak. There had been no Bishop of Cornwall since 1050, and Exeter was a long way away. Parsons were often isolated, their churches and ministry neglected. John Wesley saw a need and visited Cornwall for the first time in 1743. His kindly reception at a wayside cottage near Altarnun has become the stuff of legend. Cornwall took to Wesley like nowhere else. His message of personal redemption by faith, the Amazing Grace that saved a soul like me, went straight to the heart, as did the hymns of his brother Charles. Wesley's aim was to revitalise the Church of England from within, after his death in 1791 Methodist chapels were built in their hundreds and thousands. Further splits meant more chapels, and soon almost every settlement, every wayside, could show a chapel of some sort.

▼ **Below**: *Ebenezer Chapel at Ebenezer, Cornwall. Also closed.*

The customary plaque in the gable says Ebenezer Bible Christian 1859. The Bible Christians were an offshoot of Methodism. It is a fine building, strong

but plain, and immediately recognisable as a chapel. Surprisingly, perhaps, it is listed, but it is closed, like so many. Doors and windows have all been blocked, but a couple of air conditioners and a smart extension and entrance to one side show that, although its original function is lost, the building at least has found a new use. One of Cornwall's new industries, Tulip, is across the road and the lost chapel is now their laboratory and teaching facility.

The fine Wesleyan chapel of 1880 at Constantine on the Lizard has found a more public-spirited use. Built of the silvery granite that was extensively quarried in the parish, it was once the centre of village life, but support dwindled and eventually it was forced to close. Too big for a single dwelling, its future didn't look good, but in 1998 the specially formed Constantine Enterprises Company bought the building. Now called the Tolmen Centre, after a famous (but destroyed) granite boulder, it is now a social and entertainment centre offering meals, films, theatre, music – in fact anything at all. The ancillary rooms at the side are used as a local museum and archive centre. In the process, every internal feature that was listed in 1968, save 'unfortunately' the seats in the upper gallery, has been lost. Money has been found for a good kitchen and a toilet extension, but there is still a long way to go. The whole thing is run entirely by volunteers, and therefore dependent upon practical goodwill as well as selling tickets and filling seats. The success of a venture like this always lies on something of a knife edge.

Bethesda is named after the pools of Bethesda, a place of healing, in the old city of Jerusalem. St John's gospel, chapter five describes a place with five colonnades where sick people gathered in the shade, and where Jesus told a crippled man to 'take up your bed and walk'. John's description of the place, long thought to be allegorical, has now been confirmed by archaeology. It was the Temple of Serapis/Aesculapius, with a spine wall between the two pools and colonnades all round. The place is associated with the Byzantine church of St Anne and the birthplace of Mary.

Bethesda is a common chapel name. There are Bethesda chapels in Conwy, Amlwch, Mold, Blaenau Ffestiniog – and Hanley, but the town of Bethesda in Snowdonia takes its very name from the chapel. This is a tough quarrying town strung out along Telford's A5 and straggling up the mountainside towards the apocalyptic depths of Penrhyn slate quarry. A place of rushing streams, rocks, frowning peaks, grinding quarry lorries, and late snow. The Holyhead Road, and the Menai and Conwy bridges that highlight it, were surveyed by Thomas Telford in 1811 and built 1815–32. In 1820, at a bend in the road, Bethesda Independent chapel was built. In due course the town that developed there took its name from the chapel. As the town grew the chapel was enlarged in 1840, and again in 1872–5 (architect Richard Owens). The parish church only followed in 1855. Standing right in the middle of town, the chapel's grand stuccoed Italianate front proclaims the name BETHESDA.

In its day Bethesda town was famous for its chapels. Fifteen chapels and four churches competed for the 3,000 quarry workers, enginemen, their families and dependants. Two other big chapels remain. Bethania Independent, built of red brick and what looks like greenish-yellow terracotta, and dated 1885 and 1936; architect Rev Thomas Thomas. The chapel shows no signs of life, or death. Jerusalem Calvinistic Methodist chapel is magnificent. It was designed by T. Evans in 1842 and remodelled in 1872–5 by Richard Davies. Standing behind the town park war memorial, it is fronted by an unusual wide-arched porch. The galleried interior sweeps up in fourteen tiers of seating to the great roundel of the ceiling. When a building such as this is full, the attention of many hundreds of people focused on the fiery eloquence of a single minister, or when the whole auditorium raises the roof in song, there is nothing more uplifting. But a congregation of even a hundred is lost in such a space, conscious only of the great emptiness, the gathering dust of the vast gallery, the mocking splendour of the array of organ pipes.

Bethesda chapel is effectively lost. Closed in 1998, it has been converted into flats. The chapel noticeboard remains, but displays no service times or events. Just a row of doorbells and letterboxes. Bethesda chapel, the town's very *Fons et Origo*, plays no further part in the public life of the town. In fact,

there is nothing to be said about it except to note the façade and the name. Next to total loss, conversion to flats is the worst option because nothing is left but the exterior shell.

Bethesda chapel, in Albion Street, Hanley (Methodist New Connexion), long closed and all but derelict, entered the national consciousness with the BBC television series *Restoration* in 2003. Although beaten into first place by Victoria Baths in Manchester, the effort of presenting it and the resulting publicity was enough to stimulate the preparation of a viable scheme and for restoration work to begin. The designation of a cultural quarter around the chapel, museum and library provided an extra fillip. Work continues.

The death of John Wesley in 1791 marked the end of unity among Methodists. A dispute over the relative importance of ministers and lay people led to the Methodist New Connexion breakaway, which was joined by Job Ridgway and William Smith of Hanley in 1797. The chapel was established close to Ridgway's Bell Pottery, which stood where the Potteries Museum is now.

Hanley's Bethesda has grown in many stages. A coach-house on Albion Street was first used for worship, seating 150. It was taken down and rebuilt, with room for 600, in 1798. Extended at the back in 1811 to accommodate 1,000 seats, by 1819 it had to be extended even further. Now the building could hold up to 3,000, a huge space. The roof span of 66 feet was set by the length of American timbers

▲ **Above**: *Bethesda New Connexion Chapel at Hanley. The grand front, and the even grander interior.*

that could be brought, the length of a boat on the Trent & Mersey Canal, limited by the locks, being 70 feet. The splendid acoustic properties of the vast interior, which meant that a single speaker could hold a vast congregation spellbound, were aided by the unusually curved back wall. Finally, in 1859 a grand Corinthian front was added by the architect Robert Scrivenor. It is interesting that, as in Catherine Street chapel in Frome, the impressive public statement came last.

Bethesda in Hanley was much more than a chapel for Sunday worship. It supported its people through life and death. There was a large graveyard, now a public park, and burial vaults underneath the chapel for those who could afford it. There was a bank for members of the congregation. A large and handsome Sunday school bounded the graveyard, and there were rooms for the numerous weekly classes, band practices, prayer meetings and social occasions.

In 1907 and 1932 the reunions of Methodist congregations took away the need for competing chapels, which began the long decline. In 1912 the burial ground closed.

In 1935 there were grand plans to turn the building into a mission centre – but it didn't happen. By the 1940s there were only 150 regular worshippers in, let us remind ourselves, a building designed for 3,000. The 1950s saw some revival, but the building was deteriorating, and in 1972 part of the ceiling fell. Repairs were made but they were ineffective. Bethesda chapel in Hanley closed on 29 December 1985.

No building can be left disused and empty for long without suffering, and the building became considerably dishevelled. A trust was formed in 1994 but was unable to raise sufficient cash, and the chapel remained empty. In 2002 it was taken into care by the Historic Chapels Trust, and at last repair and restoration could begin. Phase 1 was completed in 2007, phase 2 in 2011. It is clear that a full restoration will be a long and expensive business. What is not clear is what the purpose of this great building will be.

DISSENTING CATHEDRALS: HECKMONDWIKE AND CLECKHEATON

Not cathedrals, of course, for there are no bishops. But cathedral-like in ambition and scale and in relation to their respective towns.

The demise of coal and its concomitant industries has allowed the West Yorkshire towns, once heroically black, to be cleaned. The Yorkshire stone is revealed as a beautiful honey-gold, but something else is lost: a drama, the strength of a velvet black silhouette against the northern sky. In fact buildings like this were designed to go black, with bold modelling and plenty of texture, and their detailing can look rather coarse when they are cleaned.

The Upper Independent chapel at Heckmondwike was designed by Arthur Stott, and built in 1890. It is a gigantic structure in the Baroque style, fronted by an overbearing portico of giant Corinthian columns. The gallery staircases on each side are surmounted by domes, one higher than the other because it is raised on a lantern. The imbalance is perfectly effective on the steeply sloping street. Sides and back are, as usual, plain, but of redoubtable size, and the chapel is surrounded

by a spacious but neglected graveyard. Next door is the Independent Day and Sabbath Schools building, dated 1858. Plain and unassuming in comparison, it nevertheless presents a fine five-bay front to the world, with a boldly carved flourish and inscription in the pediment.

The chapel's interior was magnificent. Under a vast coffered ceiling the pews rose rank upon rank, curving round elegantly to fit the curve of the gallery. A recess at the far end housed a splendid organ, in front of which was the elaborate raised dais for the minister and elders.

It was all too much. By the 1960s the congregation had retreated to the school in the winter months, and in 1976 they abandoned the great chapel altogether. Permission was sought to demolish it and realise the value of the land. Thanks to an intervention by the Victorian Society, the chapel and school were belatedly listed, and permission was refused. Now the case was taken to appeal, but the inspector still ruled in favour of preservation, stating that 'the appellants should make strenuous efforts to find a suitable use for this splendid church'.

No strenuous efforts were made, and the building stood empty and deteriorating for another few decades, a monument to the declining fortunes and aspirations of the town. Finally, however, a rescue of sorts has come to pass.

◀ Opposite page:
Heckmondwike. The Upper Independent Chapel is closed, its interior lost. The adjacent school soldiers on.

▲ Above: *The Upper Independent Chapel in its former glory days.*

In 2013, remorselessly cleaned and still partly scaffolded, the great chapel was undergoing conversion to flats. Not a wonderful solution, giving nothing to the community and involving loss of the internal space, but better than total loss. The school next door, still blackened and unrestored, is today's Upper Independent chapel.

Providence chapel in neighbouring Cleckheaton is a truly amazing building. 'Glory to God in the Highest' declares the cartouche in the pediment, 'and in Earth Peace, Goodwill toward Men'. Designed by Lockwood & Mawson in the late 1850s, it presents a frontage of great power. An immense pediment, heavily bracketed, stands over an open arcade of five equal arches on giant Corinthian columns framed by strongly rusticated cheeks. The whole is raised several steps, though it faces directly on to a busy road, which makes full appreciation difficult. The sides, relatively plain as usual, are a full nine bays long and reveal a complete extra storey underneath.

Providence chapel, closed in 1991, has found a different fate to others. In 2002 it was opened by the Duke of Kent as the Aakash Halal Restaurant, billing itself as 'The Largest Indian Restaurant in the World'. Which may well be true, for

◀ **Above left**: *Providence Chapel at Cleckheaton.*

▲ **Above**: *Providence Chapel in its second life as a halal restaurant.*

it is licensed to seat 850 diners and on a weekday can offer a buffet of fifty-two dishes plus a chocolate fountain.

Kitchens, food stores and laundry are in the cavernous basement. The great auditorium is busy during the day with the bustle of preparation and hums with conversation at night. A band may be playing on the dais, or a Bollywood movie flickering on the screens. Everything chapel-like has gone, but the enormous galleried space is still there, and filled every day with life. It seems somehow suitable.

CHAPTER 9

BLITZED

The devastated Coventry Cathedral, seen from the surviving steeple.

The word blitz is British shorthand, borrowed from the German *Blitzkrieg*, to denote the German air attacks on British cities during the eight or nine months between September 1940 and May 1941.

Air attack was tried in the First World War and found to be surprisingly effective. The bombing of enemy cities, with no respect for the distinction between combatants and civilians, was a major feature of the Second World War. We were all in the front line now.

After a year of 'phoney war', the Blitz of London started in earnest on 7 September 1940. Waves of bombers attacked London every day for seven weeks, and then repeatedly for another seven months, though RAF success in the Battle of Britain had by then resulted in a change of German policy from daylight to night raids. The attack was at its most intense in November and December 1940, bringing widespread destruction and loss of life. The single worst day was 19 December 1940, when nearly 3,000 people were killed.

In November 1940 the Luftwaffe broadened their attack to target other industrial cities and ports as well – Liverpool, Manchester, Glasgow, Swansea, Plymouth, Bristol, Portsmouth, Hull. Manchester was attacked for twelve hours on the night of 22–23 December. Photographs and eyewitness accounts give a flavour of the mood during that long night, when grief and despair were mixed with resignation, surprising optimism and occasional exhilaration. The venerable Cross Street chapel was completely burnt out and subsequently demolished. The Dean of Manchester, Dr Garfield Williams, captured something of the mood, seeing his cathedral that night newly revealed as 'a thing of entrancing, shocking, devastating beauty. All around, instead of hideous ugliness, there were flames shooting, apparently, hundreds of feet into the sky.' The wind was 'so filled with sparks as to give the effect of golden rain. The roar of the flames was terrific. There was "t'owd church", a fairy-like, scintillating thing in the midst of a blaze of fire.' At 6 a.m. the cathedral received a direct hit. The whole expanse of lead roof was lifted and dropped again; every window was blown out, the furnishings scattered in bits. The medieval choir stalls fell forward against each other, and the north-east corner of the building had simply disappeared.

Today the cathedral stands fully restored, although the drama and trial of that night are remembered in Margaret Traherne's Fire window. Perhaps ironically, that window was badly damaged when an IRA bomb exploded in the city in June 1996.

◀ **Left**: *John Piper painted St Michael's Cathedral on 15 November 1940, when the ruin was still hot.*

▼ **Below**: *Basil Spence's proposal for a new Coventry cathedral alongside the ruins of the old.*

COVENTRY

Three spires grace the skyline of Coventry. The two tallest, visible for miles, belong to the churches of Holy Trinity and St Michael, which lie almost side by side in the centre of town. The larger of the two, St Michael, was one of our great parish churches, stately and proud, like Yarmouth, Kendal or St Mary Redcliffe in Bristol. In 1918 it was chosen to become the cathedral of a new diocese, with a newly created bishop and hierarchy, to serve the people of Coventry and a populous chunk of the West Midlands.

The city of Coventry suffered aerial bombardment on the night of 14–15 November 1940. An advance squadron appeared first, setting down marker fires, and then hundreds of German bombers attacked the city in waves, returning to France to refuel and re-arm before resuming the attack. High explosives disrupted the water mains and telephone lines, and incendiaries set fire to buildings. The attack continued all night. When the all-clear was sounded the following morning, 4,300 homes had been destroyed, more than 500 people killed and 800 badly injured, and the compact centre of the city was more or less wiped out.

Firewatchers, armed with buckets, water, sand and a rudimentary telephone system, were stationed on the roofs of both churches. Thanks to their superhuman efforts, Holy Trinity was saved in spite of the incendiaries raining down and fires raging all around, but the team on the roof of St Michael's was overwhelmed. Fire took hold and the church burnt out of control. Lead melted and the roof fell, setting fire to everything within. The intense heat of the burning furnishings destroyed the integrity of the stone piers. By morning nothing was left amidst the rubble, twisted metal and ash except the outer walls and, miraculously, the tower and spire, still intact.

John Piper, who was serving as a war artist in nearby Northampton, arrived later in the day on 15 November. He recalled: 'Roads blocked, warehouses still burning ... that strange new smell that this war has produced – mixture of saturated burnt timber and brick dust with the emanation from cellars and hidden places. The ruined cathedral ... still hot and wet from the fire and water.' Not wishing to seem to take advantage of others' misery, he found a surviving upstairs window to sketch from. In spite of the catastrophic devastation, a secretary had arrived as usual and was at work in the same room: people really were keeping calm and carrying on. In this first painting the remaining traceries of the church seem to shimmer in the rising heat, the walls to glow.

Even as the wreckage was being cleared away, salvaged stones were set up to form a makeshift altar in the ruins. Two beams of charred and blackened timber were roughly wired together to make a cross. The words FATHER FORGIVE appeared on the wall of the apse, where they are now deeply carved. Two small crypts which had survived the bombing, and the porch with its vaulted roof, were immediately pressed into service. Three of the iron spikes which had served to cramp the roof timbers were forged into a portable cross of nails. So the work of the cathedral carried on.

A great church was lost, but in its place something more powerful had come into being, proclaiming a message of the utmost importance not just locally, but universally. In its utter ruin the cathedral of Coventry had found a new role, a new ministry for peace and forgiveness, that would prove to be felt worldwide.

In 1947 it was decided that a new cathedral must be built, and in 1950 the competition conditions were issued. In October 1950 a young architect, Basil Spence, intending to enter the competition, drove down from Edinburgh to see the site. He recalled that it was 'one of the most deeply stirring and moving days I have ever spent. In those few moments the idea of the design was planted. In essence it has never changed.' Within twenty-four hours he had produced a sketch plan. 'I saw the old Cathedral as standing for Sacrifice ... and knew that my task was to design a new one which would stand for the triumph of the Resurrection.' His was the only entry that proposed retaining the ruined cathedral as it was, and it contained almost all the essentials of the new cathedral that was to arise beside the ruins of the old. Not a parish church cathedral like the lost St Michael's (though it was no bigger), nor a Gothic one, but a true cathedral for the post-war age.

The story of the creation of the new Coventry Cathedral is an inspiring one. None of the decisions was easy, but there is no doubt that Basil Spence was inspired, and this drove the project along. Piper's paintings of the blitzed cathedral, which hung in the chapter room where the designs were debated, played a significant role in the acceptance of Spence's design. The paintings might be described as figurative, in that the scene was perfectly recognisable, but abstracted in the overlay of blocks of colour. Basil Spence's cathedral might likewise be described as traditional, in that its form is recognisable, but abstracted away from traditional style. The result is a building firmly rooted in the 1950s, just like the rebuilt city centre. Materials were in short supply, money was tight, but the desire was for something new.

Knowing the way that an architect's vision can be diluted by ongoing economies and argumentative committees, Spence made sure that the commissions for all the essential artworks such as the glass and the tapestry were in place and in progress as the building work proceeded. The result is a snapshot of the best British art at the time, or indeed European art, because the cathedral's ministry of peace attracted artists and donations from far and wide. In its way it is a period piece.

The new cathedral was consecrated on 25 May 1962, in the presence of Queen Elizabeth. Her father, George VI, had visited the ruined city and cathedral to express the sympathy of the nation just two days after the destruction of the old. On that same day, 25 May, Benjamin Britten's newly commissioned *War Requiem* was performed in the cathedral. In an unforgettable moment, the German baritone Deitrich Fischer-Dieskau sang Wilfred Owen's words, 'I am the enemy you killed, my friend'. An immensely powerful plea for peace and reconciliation, it set the tone for the new and international ministry that Coventry Cathedral plays to this day.

The fire-bombing of the city of Coventry opened up a whole new dimension of warfare, which was to bring about a pattern of outrage and retaliation that culminated in the destruction of Dresden in 1945. There was, and still remains, a lot of healing to be done. German students and volunteers have come to Coventry to help with the reconstruction, and Coventry people have gone to Dresden.

Although linked in misfortune, the path of reconstruction that the two cities have followed is strikingly different. Coventry Cathedral was built anew, straight away, in spite of the austere conditions of post-war Britain. It was built to a radically new modernist design and filled with contemporary artworks. The ruined Frauenkirche at Dresden had to wait half a century before anything was done. Then, after the reunification of Germany, it was rebuilt as close as possible to what it had been. Same stone, same techniques, same design. While Coventry Cathedral will always tell of the ordeal of the city in 1940 and the wish for something new that followed it, Dresden's Frauenkirche recreates once more the golden age of the Baroque with no reference either to 1945 or to 2005. The cities are still linked, however. The golden cross for the reconstructed Frauenkirche of Dresden was made in Britain by the son of one of the RAF crew who bombed Dresden. A dazzling object standing taller than a man, it was exhibited in Coventry before being sent to Germany and hoisted up before huge crowds on to the 'stone bell' that once more completes the famous skyline of Dresden.

LONDON, 29 NOVEMBER 1940

The famous photograph of the dome of St Paul's riding high and serene and apparently untouched over the roiling smoke and flame of the burning city remains one of the abiding images of the war.

The nightly blitz that commenced on Sunday, 29 December 1940 was concentrated on the square mile in the City of London. About a third of the buildings in the City were lost in that single night, and almost all of the City churches were damaged. The litany of burnt-out churches, most of them by Christopher Wren, is like a tolling bell: St Lawrence Jewry, St Mary le Bow, St Bride Fleet Street, St Andrew Holborn and St Andrew by the Wardrobe, St Mary Aldermanbury, St Stephen Coleman Street, St Dunstan in the East, St Vedast Foster, St Giles Cripplegate. The exquisite domed church of St Mildred Bread Street, which had kept all its original furnishings, was a particularly grievous loss. Only a few escaped almost unscathed, among them St Mary Abchurch. St Mary at Hill escaped unharmed, but was burnt out in 1988.

The tiny church of St Ethelburga Bishopsgate survived both the Great Fire and the Blitz, only to be blown to pieces by the IRA on 24 April 1993, as recounted on page 162. Sometimes the tower survived, and stands alone: St Augustine with St Faith, St Alban Wood Street, St Dunstan in the East. Many have been rebuilt but have lost much of their essential City character, St Mary le Bow and St Bride Fleet Street to name two.

The Wren church of Christchurch Newgate was one of his biggest, and was richly furnished. After the fire of 1666 Wren made a master plan for a new rectilinear city, but commercial pressure won out, as always, and the city was rebuilt on its old crooked ways. This meant that most of Wren's new churches had to be fitted into awkward and irregular sites. Not so Christchurch, which was unusually spacious and regular in its plan. This is because its site, by the New Gate just inside the City wall, was that of the medieval friary of the Franciscans: the Greyfriars. Wren's church stood upon the chancel of the Greyfriars' church, with its fine west tower upon the foundations of their central tower. The rectangular space of their

nave was kept as the new churchyard. The medieval cloister and its ancillary buildings had become Christ's Hospital School, founded by Edward VI. The children of the school in their blue coats and yellow stockings filled the capacious galleries of the church, until in 1902 it moved out to Horsham in Sussex.

A drawing of Christchurch after the inferno of that night shows one of the arcades still precariously standing, with its clerestory, and even part of the west gallery, but the ruined bits were hastily cleared away leaving only the fine tower and the outer walls. Of the fittings only the font cover survived. The shell of the church was further humiliated in 1962 when the east and south-east walls were taken down for road widening. This left the body of the church open to the world, a meaningless fragment. In 2002, however, the roads were redesigned and the missing walls were reinstated as a low stubs, waist-high, so that the church has at least regained its essential shape even though the pavement still goes through the eastern bay.

The present site is better than one might expect, offering again a pleasant oasis in the rush and hubbub of the city. The steeple and north side of the church are there, the south side half there. The other walls are represented by the rebuilt stubs, but they are at least of the right thickness and have their buttresses. The missing columns of the arcades are now represented by rose pergolas, the aisles by flagged paths, the blocks of pews by rectangular flowerbeds. The ghost of Christchurch lives again as a creative garden. The site of the Greyfriars' nave, which became Wren's churchyard, is still open and

green. The faceless offices which were built around it have at least provided covered cloister walks. So the church, though lost, is still a place with a name and a character.

Bomb damage to buildings was often exaggerated. They were frequently reported as destroyed, and then cleared away in a hurry by unskilled servicemen, when in fact they could have been saved. Churches especially are robust buildings, and it is surprising what can be recovered.

Temple Church in Bristol was hit and burnt out on the night of 24–25 November 1940 but its precariously leaning tower survives, still leaning to this day, and so do the outer walls. Out of the wreckage was pulled a beautifully delicate medieval chandelier, now in the cathedral. A week later, on 2 December, All Saints Clifton was hit and burnt out, leaving walls and tower standing and the furnishings wrecked but not destroyed. This was an exceptionally fine church by G.E. Street, but it was almost totally cleared away and is lost. Today a new church stands on the site, with only the base of the tower and a rebuilt doorway to tell of its predecessor.

▼ **Below**: *Recording wartime damage.*

▶ **Opposite**: *The wrecked village church of Chilvers Coton, 1941.*

OFF-TARGET: CHILVERS COTON

German aim was surprisingly poor, and there are many stories of stray bomb damage in unlikely places. On the evening of 24 November 1940 a parachute mine drifted quietly down upon the south Cheshire village of Bunbury, far from any intended target. Tangled in some wires, it exploded outside the north-east corner of the church, destroying a row of houses, though mercifully causing no loss of life, and badly damaging the fine Cheshire church of St Boniface. The broad windows on the south and east were all blown out, their traceries falling into the church. The roofs were unseated and had to be hastily lightened for fear of pushing out the walls, leaving the church open to the weather.

Today there is surprisingly little to tell of what must surely have been the most dramatic event ever to hit that sleepy place. The 1950s roofs and glass of the church tell their tale to those who have eyes to see, and so does the strange gap in the fabric of the village, but it is odd that, while there are memorials to everything from the fourteenth-century founder to the millennium, there is no memorial to the Blitz. There is hardly a mention in the guide book, and no marker where the bomb went off. Perhaps sometimes we prefer to forget.

The midland town of Nuneaton came under intensive air attack on the evening of 17 May 1941. An eloquent relic of that night is the air raid warden's logbook, which is preserved at the town's museum. As the night progressed and the bomb reports came in one after another the warden's handwriting, neat to start with, deteriorates until it is almost impossible to read. More than in any of the words it tells how desperate the situation was.

A short walk out of town is the village of Chilvers Coton and the church of All Saints. It now quite a suburban place, but its village life and characters in the nineteenth century were recorded by Mary Ann Evans, alias the novelist George Eliot, who was born nearby, baptised in the church and brought up in the village.

In the early hours of 17 May 1941 a rain of stray incendiaries set fire to the church and burnt it out. The fire provided a target, and a little later, while it was still burning, a high-explosive bomb landed immediately outside. The explosion brought down the roofs and outer walls, but at the same time blew out the fire in the tower before it could reach the bells, which were saved. Little else was left, however; only the gable walls at each end and part of the chancel. The wreck was photographed and painted by the artist Miles Sharp and others.

After the debris was cleared thoughts turned to rebuilding the church. Labour could not be spared, so an experimental permit was issued for German prisoners of war from 196 POW camp Nuneaton (Arbury Hall) to come and help with the work. Behaviour on both sides was carefully monitored, recording 'a good deal of trouble from children and girls in the early days', but the scheme was judged successful enough to continue. In fact it went on even after 1945; the Church was much exercised over the moral issue of prisoners being held after the end of the war.

The design was made by a local architect, H.N. Jepson. Like Basil Spence at Coventry he had no thought of recreating the medieval architecture, proposing instead a modern building for post-war Britain. The style might be termed Utility

▼ *Below left: German POWs at work on the reconstruction.*

▼ *Below right: The reconstructed church is much wider than the old, its design typical of the 1940s and 50s.*

architecture, although drawings show that Jepson initially planned something much more grandiose.

The vicar, the Revd R.T. Murray, acted at times as clerk of works, the vicarage as the design office. Materials were hard to come by, money was tight, building permits not always forthcoming. Nevertheless, building work went ahead, and the Germans were the mainstay of the rebuild and the decorative work associated with it.

The church in its big churchyard presents today an unusual picture. The tower is little changed – even the weathervane survived the Blitz. Nave and chancel have the usual pointed roofs, but they are sandwiched between very wide and flat-roofed aisles on either side, giving the church a very horizontal look. The new stonework is unconventional rubble-work, only roughly levelled and laid to course but nevertheless skilfully done. The masons were Fritz Beyer, Johann Hoffmann and Willi Schinkel, the carpenters Erwin Michel, Heinrich Hillgartner and

Rudolf Dietze. The windows are simple wide lancets plainly glazed. Inside is even more unusual, though very typical of the 1940s and 1950s. Apart from the surviving chancel and tower arches, the whole thing is constructed on the post-and-beam principle, not in the least bit Gothic. The arcades are simple square columns and flat beams. There is plenty of light and space. The aisle roofs are wide and flat, with skylights, and coffered over steel. The nave ceiling has been rebuilt to fit the surviving gable as a steel-faceted barrel with concrete panels. Only the chancel roof is wood, though again with concrete panels.

The church is brought to life by the carved decorative work carried out by Heinrich Schonmeyer (wood) and Max Hatzinger (stone). Both were highly skilled and inventive despite having to make do with reclaimed wood and stone. The font is fashioned out of the stump of a medieval pillar, its beautiful cover depicting the baptism carved out of salvaged wood. The lectern, with three carved scenes on its desk,

sits on a wrought-iron bracket slotted into what looks like the base and capital of another medieval column. The altar, made of reclaimed blocks of stone, bears a carved phoenix on its face. In the churchyard the risen Christ, sculpted by Carl Weber out of what he could find, looks benignly down on the garden of remembrance.

Without forgetting the damage caused by the POWs to Arbury Hall, which took years to restore to a habitable state, the story of the rebuilding of a church lost through enemy action by that same enemy is surely an inspiring one. It inspired both the parishioners and the prisoners who carried out the work. Heinrich Schonmeyer, whose prisoner-of-war index card is preserved at the church, is one of several who have returned to Chilvers Coton to be photographed with their work. When the rebuilt church was rededicated on Friday, 26 September 1947 the bishop called it a modern miracle.

In April 1942 came the Baedeker raids, retaliatory morale-busters aimed at the historic and cultural cities of as Bath, Canterbury, York, Exeter and Norwich. Enraged by the Allied bombing of Lübeck and Rostock, Hitler himself reputedly ordered the bombing of every town awarded three stars in Baedeker's famous travel guides. Exeter Cathedral was badly damaged, as was the monastic part of Canterbury Cathedral. York was hit on 29 April 1942, from 2.30 a.m. Ninety-two were killed, hundreds injured. The medieval and timber-framed Guildhall was completely burnt out. Next to it was St Martin-le-Grand, an ambitious church on a confined site between Coney Street and the river, with very big Perpendicular windows and fine glass. An ingenious rebuild of part of it by George Pace roofed in the north aisle and one arcade only, plus the tower. The nave was left as an open courtyard, the clerestory lost. The medieval glass of the west window had already been removed to safety, so Pace made a new window of the same size and tracery to contain it, facing the courtyard.

The year 1944 marked the appearance of the unmanned V1 flying bombs, called doodlebugs for the droning sound made by the crude pulse-jet engine. This was a Luftwaffe initiative and they could be launched from the ground or from an aircraft. Most were aimed at London but a few, for some reason, targeted Norwich, and one batch went for Manchester. They were really noisy, with a red flare at the tail. When the engine cut out you knew somebody was for it. Their accuracy was quite poor, and the RAF and AA gunners became quite good at shooting them down.

The village church of Little Chart near Ashbourne in Kent was hit on 16 August 1944 by a flying-bomb which, like so many others, fell short of its target – the result of falsified information? No lives were lost, but the church was knocked into a cocked hat. It has been left as a ruin, surrounded by its maintained graveyard. Instead, a new church designed by H. Anderson was built in 1955–6 on a different site. 'Wan neo-Gothic' John Newman calls it, in brick with a tiled roof, and quite domestic looking. It does have a tower and bells, though.

Soon after the V1s came the lethal and terrifying – but mercifully too late – V2 rockets. This was an army initiative, unlike the Lufwaffe's V1s. Launched from France or the Low Countries, each missile took only four minutes to reach its target, descending at supersonic speed and landing and exploding without warning. They were also quite inaccurate, and quite a few failed.

The first V2 landed in Chiswick in west London on 8 September 1944, killing three. Later that same day a second hit a crowded Woolworths on Deptford High Street: 240 were killed, many injured. On 4 January 1945 a V2 hit Dalston library, destroying it completely. Two librarians and several children were among the dead. The neighbouring church of Holy Trinity served as a morgue.

A V2 knocked out the Jacobean Charlton House in Greenwich.

A massive V2 manufacturing and launching site at La Coupoule in France, constructed by slave labour, was luckily knocked out by the RAF before it could become operational. It has recently opened as a museum. Casualties among the slave labour were greater than those caused by strikes.

St Ethelburga, Bishopsgate. The little medieval church survived both the Great Fire and the Blitz.

ST ETHELBURGA BISHOPSGATE, 24 APRIL 1993

The medieval church of St Ethelburga, on the northern fringe of the City of London, was the most humble and the cutest of the City churches, its diminutive front peeping out between its overblown neighbours. It never had a proper tower, merely a little wooden turret perched on a flat gable, and inside was just a crooked nave and a single narrow aisle. Beyond the east wall was a tiny churchyard.

St Ethelburga always was one of the smallest, but by the 1930s it had become comically dwarfed by the towering office blocks that sandwiched it on either side. Almost all the windows had been blocked by them, so that a brick clerestory had to be raised over the arcade to give at least some daylight. To make matters worse, the churchwardens, to supplement the church's slender income, had allowed a pair of shops to be built in front. Nothing of the church was now visible now except a doorway sign, the clock and the wooden turret and weathervane peeping above the shop roofs.

St Ethelburga survived the Great Fire of 1666 which had destroyed so much of the city. It survived the Blitz, which devastated swathes of what was left. But in mid-morning 24 April 1993 – a Saturday – a heavy truck was parked on the street immediately outside. Two men got out and were picked up by a car, stolen like the lorry, which quickly drove off. Then the coded IRA warnings started to come in. Underneath a thin layer of tarmac the lorry was packed with high explosive. At 10.27 a.m. it went off.

The damage was enormous, the human toll mercifully light. Steel- and concrete-framed buildings had every window and fixture blown out, but St Ethelburga, only 7 metres from the lorry and bomb, was blown to smithereens. Where the church had been there remained simply a hole.

As the salvage operation swung into action it was discovered, surprisingly, that something of the church had survived after all. The three arches of the medieval arcade were still standing, and so was much of the east wall. The stones of the western arch were scattered but recoverable, and so were some of the timbers. Even the weathervane was recovered, albeit a trifle bent.

What now? A faction within the Church was in favour of selling the site and realising the profit for use elsewhere, but given the survival of so much, in spite of first appearances, this seemed heartless. The Company of Clothworkers gave money towards rebuilding, and since 2002 St Ethelburga is once more complete and open as a centre for reconciliation and peace. It looks the same from outside, though minus the shops which were taken down in the late 1930s, but is transformed within. The pews have gone, and so has Ninian Comper's beautiful if traditional screen. Instead we have free-flowing space, with a temporary structure within the reconstructed volume to house meetings and events. The old exterior, a new interior. Perhaps that is the spirit of our time.

▶ **Right:** *St Ethelburga. Bombed out by the IRA in 1993, and for a while given up for lost.*

▼ **Overleaf:** *Bishopsgate April 1993, with a hole where St Ethelburga had been.*

CHAPTER 10

HUBRIS

The dictionary defines hubris as overweening pride leading to nemesis. As the proverb has it, pride comes before a fall.

Churches have been lost over the centuries for many reasons, but some, with hindsight, seem to have been doomed from the start. Indeed, churches are especially afflicted with built-in problems, because the urge and ambition that created them outstrip practical sense. A sensible builder will always make sure that the finances are in place before starting, but the builders of a church may well trust in God to provide. A prudent builder, knowing the limitations of materials and the worst that the weather can do, will stick to tried and trusted methods, but a church builder, desirous of building ever higher and more ethereal, will push material considerations to the limit and beyond. Ongoing care and maintenance is an unglamorous subject that is often disregarded, but particularly so in a building like a church of impractical extremes, however beautiful. Simple jobs like clearing the gutters can be neglected because they are too hard to get at. Dry rot has proved to be a particular curse in Victorian churches whose design makes day-to-day maintenance difficult. And to these built-in problems, of cash, structure and maintenance, we can perhaps add a sort of spiritual weariness, a fatal ennui, that can come upon church builders, akin to that which can afflict a collector who realises that when the collection is complete life will no longer be worth living. What is it all for? Does it matter in the grand scheme of things whether this great project is completed or not? It can result in work being abandoned half finished, perhaps with only half a nave, or no proper west front, or only a stump of the intended steeple. Cologne Cathedral was left like this for centuries.

The twentieth century, and particular the 1960s, offered architects a whole new box of tricks and new opportunities for hubris. Steel, reinforced concrete, sheet glass, mastics and silicones promised an architecture without limits. The prospect of being able to build spectacularly, but also quickly and cheaply, bypassing the traditional skills, was intoxicating. It opened up many exciting new opportunities to build in failure.

The two twentieth-century cathedrals of Liverpool, Catholic and Protestant, illustrate the point perfectly. The Anglican cathedral on its dominant site was started in 1904 to the design of a young architect, Giles Gilbert Scott. Through two world wars and Liverpool's fall from prosperity to depression he was able to see the slow building of the cathedral through until his death in 1960. During that time, however, the design changed radically; the winning 1904 design had twin towers

Booton Church. The unconventional west front, with its towers set diagonally.

over the transepts for instance, like Exeter, where the finished cathedral has a single mighty tower over an enormous central space. Its Gothic style and stone construction became old-fashioned even as it was rising ('well, they're a long time knocking that old church down' heard from a passer-by), and the last phase was finished in 1978 to a more economical specification using fibreglass instead of stone for the vault. It is an enormous building, highly impractical in many respects, and may prove difficult to maintain in the long run.

The Roman Catholic cathedral was intended to outshine it in every way. Designed by Edwin Lutyens and started in 1933, it was going to be bigger even that St Peter's in Rome, with an enormous dome. Just half of the crypt was completed by the time war broke out, its magnificent workmanship demonstrating what a stupendous building it would have been.

When work started again in 1962 it was to a radical modernist design by Frederick Gibberd. Gone were all ambitions of vast size and imperishable masonry. Instead the Catholics stole a march by building a complete cathedral in just five years for little more than a million pounds.

It was stunning, but like so many 1960s buildings the new cathedral leaked. Aluminium cladding detached itself from the roof, mosaic from the concrete ribs. The diocese sued the architect, and a £3 million repair and makeover was completed in 2009.

It will be interesting to see how these two buildings, hubristic in their utterly different ways, survive in the future.

◀ **Left**: *Booton, the angelic interior.*

▼ **Overleaf**: *Booton Church, south view. The window tracery was taken from J.S. Crowther's textbook, see pp 23 and 24.*

ST MICHAEL THE ARCHANGEL, BOOTON, NORFOLK

The Revd Whitwell Elwin was a notable representative of that honourable British type, the eccentric country parson. A man of independent means and grand ideas, he was nevertheless happy to spend the last fifty years of his life in the small village of Booton, not far from Reepham in rural north-east Norfolk. An early curacy at Hemington with Hardington near Frome in Somerset had given him the opportunity to see the eccentric Christ Church in the village of Rode, with its extraordinary twin steeples, which had been built by the Revd Charles Daubeny in 1824. In 1876, buoyed perhaps by an offer of £1,500 a year towards the project from a lady friend, he determined to rebuild his own church in magnificent style.

Elwin was not an architect, but he designed it all himself. He had considerable trouble with the technicalities, but with the help of the measured drawings of medieval examples that Victorian architects liked to publish he was able to build a church whose grandeur and originality rivalled, in its eccentric way, even such celebrated medieval neighbours as Salle and Cawston.

His most eye-catching feature is the twin west towers, attenuated and transparent, which are placed at an angle of 45 degrees to the rest. This is a most uncomfortable conceit, radically upsetting the geometry; the idea came perhaps from the abbey church of St Ouen at Rouen, which does the same thing. Between them, balanced on the gable, rises a tall three-stage pinnacle or turret like a minaret. Outsize pinnacles or spirelets sprout on the chancel arch and east gable as well. A spacious three-bay vestry juts out from the south side, almost like the start of a cloister, and indeed the extra buttresses that flank the chancel door make one wonder if he did intend such a thing.

The interior is all angels. Angels with outstretched wings hover overhead on every hammerbeam, and sweetly feminine angels throng the stained glass of the windows. Elwin's nature was evidently not of a didactic kind; he preferred angelic village maidens – they are said to be portraits – to biblical instruction in his stained glass.

When the Revd Elwin died on 1 January 1900 he left to the care of his scattered parish a church that was far too grand for their needs. It was difficult to heat and expensive to maintain. Declared redundant, it was taken over by the Churches Conservation Trust in 1987. The CCT aims to keep the building sound and weatherproof, and if possible open, but not much more. In a time of economic austerity this cannot be guaranteed in perpetuity unless a benign use for the building can be found.

Incidentally, Christ Church at Rode, a building 'spirited to the point of recklessness', was itself closed in 1995. It now houses a violin maker, serving as dwelling, workshop and performance space in one.

CATHOLIC APOSTOLIC CHURCH, GORDON SQUARE, BLOOMSBURY, LONDON

The Catholic Apostolic Church had its origin in 1832 when the 'shooting star' evangelist Henry Irving was evicted with his flock from their church in Regent Square. Irving preached the imminent second coming of Christ, and his services had degenerated into what some saw as apocalyptic chaos, as hearers went into a frenzy, speaking in tongues and prophesying. After wandering in the wilderness for a while, holding services in the open air or at hired venues, they rented a former exhibition hall in Newman Street. The lease on the premises had only thirty-three years to run, but that fitted in with their millennial beliefs.

It was a strongly hierarchical organisation full of mystical symbolism. There were seven churches in London, echoing the seven churches of Asia in the Apocalypse of St John. Each was headed by an 'Angel', or heavenly messenger. Then there were twelve 'Apostles' who ministered to the twelve tribes or nationalities recognised by the church. Deacons and deaconesses were presumably meant to represent the multitude of 144,000 that were to follow.

Proposals for a grand church in Gordon Square, near the British Museum, were discussed in 1851. There were objections from within. One member protested that he would rather have 'a finished church according to our means' than a superb but unfinished

one. He was overruled, though subsequently proved
right. Others, more significantly, doubted that a
permanent building of stone was necessary if Christ's
second coming and the end of all things was truly
imminent. And a third, purely practical, remembered
that the ground was not freehold, merely leased, and
would eventually revert to the Duke of Bedford.

Nevertheless, building went ahead. The
deacons commissioned John Raphael Brandon to
build them a 'glorious structure, the noblest of
Metropolitan Churches'. Brandon was a scholar
and writer on medieval architecture but found little
success as a practising architect apart from the Gordon
Square church. In 1877, in despair at the death of
his wife and child and the failure of his career, he
committed suicide.

Cathedral-like in scale, medieval French
Gothic in style, the Catholic Apostolic Church arose
on its tight site. A lot of architectural ambition had
to be squeezed into a narrow compass. Hence the
transepts could not project beyond the rectangle, and
even the buttresses had to be tightly contained within
the building line. With a full cathedral panoply of
arcade, triforium and tall clerestory, it was faced
inside and out in golden Bath stone and vaulted at
the east end, with much rich carving.

It never was finished. The nave stops abruptly,
two bays shorter than planned, in a plain brick wall.
The central steeple, meant to soar to 300 feet, only
just clears the high roof. John Belcher, an architect
of Baroque inclinations and a member of the church,
put forward plans in 1885 to complete the building
in even more ambitious style, but nothing came of it.

In the great nave, which was intended to
hold assemblies of all seven churches, or 'Councils
of Zion', is the seat of the 'Angel', effectively the

▶ **Right**: *Incongruous in Bath
stone, the unfinished Catholic
Apostolic Church, Gordon
Square.*

death of the last Pinta Galapagós tortoise Lonesome George in 2012, it really meant the end of the species. In the 1960s the last deacon, James Lickfold, handed the church over to the Anglican Chaplaincy of the University of London. The chaplaincy was based here until 1992.

Incongruous in its sedate Georgian setting with its stout iron railings and giant plane trees, visibly unfinished, and doomed by its hierarchy and beliefs from the very start, the church is yet listed at the highest Grade I, which implies that it is here for keeps. Currently the small English Chapel is used by the 'Forward in Faith' group, and generally found open. The rest still awaits the second coming.

ST JOHN, MACCLESFIELD

On 30 June 1991 a gathering of all the churches of the Diocese of Chester was held on the Roodee, just outside the walls of the city. The occasion was a celebration of the 450th anniversary of the Diocese. Each church was encouraged to bring its church banner. It made a colourful scene. Among all the Virgin Marys, St Georges or St Christophers, one banner stood out above all the others. Instead of the titular saint it sported a jolly design of drips and buckets. Thus the parishioners of St John Macclesfield chose to celebrate the salient feature of their church.

There have been three St John's. The first, of 1873, had to come down because it had been built on the shifting sands next to the Dams Brook which winds its way through town. Fittings such as the altar and reredos were saved, and have found homes in other churches in town.

St John's no. 2 was built on a new site to serve a new estate. It was built on a piece of waste ground between the houses, just rough grass, which never looked much more than waste. Daringly modernist, it was an adventurous 1960s design by Paterson & Macauley. Shaped like a boat, the roof rose to a very tall prow at one end, swooshed down in the middle and then rose again to the stern. In plan it was diamond-shaped, more like a grounded kite. The lower two corners were curved downwards to anchor it to the ground. Indeed, the trendy chains that were meant

bishop's throne. What looks like a lower Lady Chapel was reserved for the 'Apostle' of the English tribe, so it was called the English Chapel. Next door are the 'cloisters', an ecclesiastical warren of offices and flats.

No provision had been made for the non-event of the second coming. The last Apostle of the Catholic Apostolic Church, Francis Valentine Woodhouse, died on 3 February 1901. Only an Apostle could ordain new ministers, so, like the to take off the rainwater looked rather like anchor chains. Inside, it was surprisingly spacious. Brute materials, concrete, brick and wood, were exposed, the timber-clad swoop of the roof being particularly effective. The altar, dramatically lit, stood under the highest peak of the roof. The piano, organ and choir were at the other end, at the stern so to speak, and the congregation sat in between.

The roof leaked. The local children had quickly discovered that the low corners made it quite easy to climb on to the roof, and it made a wonderful adventure playground. Made of laminated wood covered in copper sheet, it was curved in two planes like a BMX track. Riding bikes on it made for some interesting sound effects during services, but did not improve its water-resistant properties.

The other sound effect was the steady plink-plink of water filling the buckets which had to be assembled under the lower corners of the roof.

By the 1990s the swoopy timber roof was looking dull all over on the inside, and showing signs of rot. It would have been perfectly possible to repair it, and remedy its faults, though as at Liverpool Metropolitan Cathedral this would probably have been at greater cost than the original build. Nobody leapt to its defence, however; its faults outweighed its virtues. And so the decision was made. After only thirty years of life, it would have to go.

So, while St John's no. 2 was taken down, no. 3 was built alongside. The experimental nature of no. 2 was apparent in the difficulty of dismantling and disposing of its components. Long beams of reinforced concrete, fibreglass windows, the single great curved sheet of laminated timber all had to be taken down and cut up. No. 3, by Graham Holland, is conventional in structure and form, using tried and tested methods: a steel frame with brick infill and glass windows. The belfry gives it an echo of Spanish Mission style. With an attached vicarage and laid out car park it does at least look as though it is here to stay.

◀ **Opposite page**: *Catholic Apostolic Church. The throne of the 'Angel'.*

▲ **Above**: *A parish banner commemorates the drips and buckets which bedevilled so many 1960s buildings.*

OUR LADY STAR OF THE SEA AND ST WINEFRIDE, AMLWCH
(MAIR, SEREN Y MOR A SANTES WENFRED)

This episode at least has a happy ending.

The Italian architect and engineer Giuseppe Rinvolucri (1894–1963), from Piedmont, was brought to Amlwch on Anglesey during the First World War as a prisoner of war. Making himself at home, as Italian prisoners so often did, he married a Welsh girl. They had four children and settled in Glan Conwy.

During the 1930s he built several Roman Catholic churches, including those at Porthmadog, Abergele, Conwy and Ludlow. They all make extensive use of concrete, but his little church at Amlwch was by far the most adventurous. The church was built among the rocks and sand dunes outside town, originally all on its own. A base storey of local stone, with portholes, was built first to accommodate a half-sunken parish hall, and a stone frontispiece above. That was in 1932; the builder was Mr Roberts of Amlwch. Then, in 1935, a concrete beam floor was laid over it, and the main church built on top. It was carried out by Percy Iball of Rhyl. This was the tricky part of the operation, because the church takes the outlandish form of a parabolic arch, executed in concrete. Nobody in

▼ **Below**: *St John's Macclesfield. The leaky church comes down, while its successor is under construction.*

▶ **Opposite page**: *Amlwch. The stunningly restored interior of Our Lady and St Winefride, 1932–5.*

Wales had experience of any such thing. Iball recruited John Williams, joiner, to do the complicated formwork needed to support the arch until it could support itself, and with a few labourers they completed the job in about ten months. The arch butts up to the stone frontispiece at one end, and a parabolic half-cone forming the sanctuary backs on to a little sacristy of brick.

Five parabolic arches of reinforced concrete were made first, and then a thin concrete shell formed in between. There are no conventional windows at all; instead, three strips of two-inch-thick glass in star patterns punctuate the roof, plus five little star windows round the apse, and a bigger star above the west door. Nor are there any conventionally vertical walls. The parabolic roof rises direct from the floor, so the two doorways into the sacristy have to lean inwards. The concrete parabola is naked to the elements, a pure theorem, uncontained and unbuttressed, with no outer covering.

A parabola looks unstable to our unaccustomed eyes but is actually extremely strong. All the stresses are contained within the curve, so that a parabolic arch, however wide, needs no extra ties or buttressing. Gaudí knew this, as did the ancient Parthians, and so did Rinvolucri. The result is not pretty. It looks tiny from outside, but the interior, although only seven paces wide and

Amlwch. The church in the sand dunes newly restored.

eighteen long, feels surprisingly spacious, almost unlimited.

The naked parabola gave trouble in the Welsh climate from the start, much like the naked vault of Rosslyn chapel. It was a constant battle against leaks and condensation, and the vault, once painted pink, gradually sprouted a patchwork of damp stains and mould. By October 1994 the ingress of water was threatening the electrics, and the church had to be closed as unsafe. An appeal to the National Heritage Lottery Fund was refused, so the outlook seemed bleak. However, the church, unlike St John's Macclesfield, was recognised as a remarkable creation. It always had its champions, among them Simon Jenkins who included it in his *Churches, Houses and Castles of Wales* (2008), ending his account with the words, 'The church must be saved'. Improved techniques made waterproofing the concrete shell realistic. The money was found. It reopened in 2011, the exterior resealed and the interior all white.

It is a funny-looking building in its sandy car park, the top half black apart from the frontispiece, including the makeshift-looking sacristy at the back. The bottom half is painted white, and very seasidy with its portholes. The parish room is oddly reminiscent of the lower deck of a ship, with its portholes just above the waves. The church interior at the top of its steps is wonderful, a great surprise. Because it has no walls or ceiling, just a seamless curve, the space flows and

seems limitless. Seaside light from the starry windows and open door floods the entire volume, with little to distract – just the 1930s woodblock floor and good simple new furnishings.

ST PETER'S COLLEGE, CARDROSS, ARGYLL

This may be the greatest of all our lost churches. We are too close to the event to know for certain. It is certainly the most dramatically lost, although there is hope. And, bizarrely, it is the most modern.

Finding it is not easy. From Glasgow bear left at Dumbarton, following the Clyde, and the first thing you see of Cardross is the old parish church. This, as it happens, is also lost. All that is left standing is its

ANGLESEY, AMLWCH R.C. CHURCH. (UPPER) INTERIOR

head and shoulders, so to speak, the tower and west wall: a managed ruin set in a bosky churchyard with several walled mausolea for company. It was built in 1826 but bombed in 1941. Lost churches are a common sight in Scotland.

A mile or so to the north a spiked fence and DANGER notice guards, not very effectively, the abandoned demesne of Kilmahew House. Hidden and utterly ruined in these dripping woods is St Peter's Catholic College, an icon of modern architecture and an irresistible draw to vandals and graffiti artists. Estate roads wind and fork, ornamental bridges crumble. Eventually a second spiked gate and another DANGER sign bar the way. Behind, glimpsed through the luxuriant greenery like a lost Aztec temple in the jungle, are the long horizontals and Corbusian light scoops of the college. For the intrepid architectural traveller a steep but well-worn path drops to a gap in the fence, and the entrance to an extraordinary lost world, deeply sinister and yet poetically beautiful in its abject ruination.

▲ **Above**: *Amlwch. The ship-like parish room which was built under the church.*

◀ **Opposite page**: *The church when it was newly completed.*

This is a seriously scary place, heightening all the senses. Standing water and soggy debris hide potential pratfalls. Who else might be lurking there, and who might come in after you? And will the gap still be open when it is time to leave?

Yet this was and is a highly acclaimed piece of progressive architecture, award-winning in the 1960s, registered by the World Monuments Fund, and listed at the highest level. Let us search for its virtues. It certainly has drama.

St Peter's Roman Catholic College was designed by Gillespie, Kidd & Coia of Glasgow and built in 1962–8 – Jack Coia, Isi Metstein and Andy Macmillan being the executant architects. It was intended by Archbishop Scanlon of Glasgow to become the principal Catholic Seminary in west Scotland, and was planned to house up to 100 trainee priests at a time. Both the archbishop and the architects intended to make a major statement, demonstrating the vigour and modernity of the church in a time of great change. But either its optimism was misplaced or the timing of the commission and the design was highly unfortunate. Either way, it was doomed from the start.

The complex was purpose-built. This was still a time when priests were trained in semi-monastic seclusion, and when each priest was required to celebrate mass at his own altar every day. In Latin, with his back to the people. Every detail of the projected life of the community was thought out, and incorporated into the megastructure in imperishable materials. The style was the concrete modernism of the moment, the modernism of the Barbican complex or the National Theatre in London, following the late great works of Le Corbusier. St Peter's College was one of the boldest example of Brutalism in Britain, meaning that the brute materials, principally concrete, were left raw to tell their own tale.

A long concrete platform is raised over the uneven ground. Upon that base, end-to-end, are the spacious chapel, a central circulation area with steps up and down, and the equally spacious refectory. A ramp curls down behind the altar to a stepped bank of subterranean sacristies, where the elements of the mass were prepared. This is now a particularly creepy place. The teaching block was attached at right

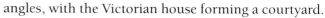

◀ **Left**: *Masterpiece or disaster? The seminary of 1962–8 stands lost and abandoned in the jungle.*

▼ **Below**: *The high altar, now smashed and despoiled, was a single piece of solid granite.*

angles, with the Victorian house forming a courtyard.

On top of chapel and refectory is the stepped ziggurat of the student study-bedrooms. The three floors step inwards on the outside, so each tier has a balcony, but they are also stepped inside to make a hollow internal ziggurat, with open galleries. All this is supported on very little, now that all the glass and wood has gone; just a few slender piloti. However, flanking the chapel on each side is the most striking feature of the complex: a battery of five cowled half-cylinders, with the appearance of hooded monks. They are meant to be mass concrete like the rest, but the cruel weather has revealed them to be merely of brick, rendered to look like concrete. These were some of the individual chapels, each one top-lit, where the young priests could celebrate the required daily mass. Something similar can be seen around the polygon of Liverpool Metropolitan Cathedral.

The centre and heart of the whole complex was the chapel. Spaciously broad but not particularly high. We are aware of the tiers of rooms overhead: brightly lit at the curved east end but with more mysterious rays of daylight illuminating the rest. It was seated college-wise, the central space stepping down like a shallow arena. Behind the altar a processional ramp curves down – as it does at Liverpool – to the sacristies below. The central altar is a single enormous chunk of natural granite: a contrast to the man-made concrete of the rest. One massive corner has been smashed off, which must have been an extremely arduous task.

The college opened in 1966. Nothing went right. The roofs leaked, mould grew. Day-to-day maintenance proved to be a nightmare. Such problems can be solved, but in Rome the deliberations of the Second Vatican Council, which concluded in 1965, had already sealed its fate. Priests were now allowed to concelebrate, that is to say the mass together at the same altar. No need for all those chapels. They were required to use the language of the people, and to face the people from behind the altar. Cardross's altars are immovable concrete, part of the structure. Priests were now encouraged to train in the community, not in an isolated seminary like this. Moreover, vocations to the priesthood were falling rapidly.

The college never attracted even half its intended numbers of students. It functioned for a mere twelve years, at the end of which there were just twenty-one in residence. It was deconsecrated and closed in 1980. After five years as a drug rehabilitation unit the place was abandoned altogether.

In 1995 Kilmahew House was set on fire and had to be demolished. Even its footprint is now lost in the vigorous greenery. Only the shallow stone stair leading to its front door tells of its existence. The rest has proved to be pretty well indestructible. All the wood has gone, and of course all the glass lies smashed underfoot. Water lies in pools, trees sprout in every crevice. The teaching block, evidently of lighter construction, looks highly unsafe. But the massive, Brutal concrete of the megastructure seems set to last until Doomsday.

So the newest is the most utterly lost. Lost in the changing doctrines of the Catholic Church, lost to the unpopularity of 1960s Brutalism, lost because the architects have thought of everything and designed it in, lost even because it is listed Category A and therefore cannot be changed. Lost in the deep woods of an abandoned country estate. But – stop press – in spring 2014 the Heritage Lottery Fund announced a record grant of £4,336,800 to restore it as 'a modernist ruin'.

The college in its present condition as a genuinely ruined ruin is undoubtedly an exciting place, an irresistible draw to adventurous teenagers, students and historians of architecture, photographers and film-makers, satanists and druggies alike. It is the perfect setting for the artists whose vivid graffiti make it a brilliant gallery of unofficial art. In its nemesis it has paradoxically achieved greatness. Like the unfinished cathedral at Oban it poses more powerful questions in failure than it would do in completion and success. But it cannot and will not stand still.

Cardross. The underground sacristy, transformed by graffiti artists into something else.

'No church will endure for ever. Yet as places go, those believed to be holy come nearer to a state of permanence than any other'

Richard Morris, *Churches in the Landscape.*

ACKNOWLEDGEMENTS

One of the rules of The Buildings of England, Scotland and Wales is that they do not include lost buildings, however intriguing. If it's gone, it has gone. So I thank the commissioning editors at Aurum Press for this opportunity to undertake some redress.

I would like to thank John Adams for the Syon connection, and for inviting us to the relaunch of the Syon Abbey Herbal on the 600th anniversary of the abbey's foundation. Belinda and Stephen King for taking me to Dunwich and Covehithe, and introducing me to Chapel Barn. To Mark Flinn in Chester, Emily and Adrian Brown in Truro for their hospitality and local knowledge. John Adams again for an expedition of Canterbury and Reculver. Ruth Shrigley and Hannah Williamson at Manchester City Art Gallery for a good look at the Piper painting of bombed-out Coventry. And Margaret the churchwarden at Chilvers Coton for digging out the wartime records.

If this book has proved anything it is that we owe special thanks to those stubborn people up and down the land who have refused, against all the odds, to allow their church to be lost. Churches have a rare knack of survival, but only if somebody loves them.

BIBLIOGRAPHY

The church, or its site, always comes first; that and local guides. But the following have proved useful.

Relevant volumes of *The Buildings of England, Scotland* and *Wales* (London: Yale)

Birch, George H. *London Churches of the XVII and XVIII Centuries* (London: Batsford, 1896).

Carley ,James P. *Glastonbury Abbey* (London: Guild, 1988).

Cobb, Gerald. *The Old Churches of London* (London: Batsford, 1941–2).

Fletcher, Hanslip. *Bombed London* (London: Cassell, 1947).

Hyde, Matthew. *J. S. Crowther, Architect* (MA thesis: Keele, 1992).

Jackson, Peter. *George Scharf's London* (London: John Murray, 1987).

Jones, Christopher. *The Great Palace - The Story of Parliament* (London: BBC, 1983)

Lambert, Nick. *Llandaff Cathedral* (Bridgend: Seren, 2010).

Longman, William. *The Three Cathedrals Dedicated to St Paul* (London: Longmans, Green, 1873).

Marshall, Brian. *Cockersand Abbey* (Blackpool: Landy, 2001).

McEwan, Richard I. *None Will Remain: Five Lost Churches in Manchester* (London: ACHS, 2014).

Morris, Richard. *Churches in the Landscape* (London: Dent, 1989).

Nash, Gerallt (ed). *Saving St Teilo's* (National Museum of Wales 2009).

Owen, D. Huw. *The Chapels of Wales* (Bridgend: Seren, 2012).

Pope-Hennessey, James. *History Under Fire* (London: Batsford, 1941).

Powell, Ken. *The Fall of Sion* (London: SAVE Britain's Heritage, 1980).

Richards, J. M. (ed). *The Bombed Buildings of Britain* (London: Architectural Press, 1947).

Schofield, John. *St Paul's Cathedral Before Wren* (Swindon: English Heritage, 2011).

Spalding, Frances. *John Piper, Myfanwy Piper* (Oxford: OUP, 2009).

Spence, Basil. *Phoenix at Coventry* (London: Geoffrey Bles, 1962).

Summerson, Henry et al. *Brougham Castle* (Location: CWAAS, 1998).

Todd, John. *Seaton Nunnery* (St Bees: Publisher, 1980).

PICTURE CREDITS

Author collection 1, 2, 11, 12-13, 17 (left and right), 18, 20-21, 22,-3, 24, 26, 27, 34-5, 39, 42-3, 49, 50, 51, 53, 57, 58, 60-61, 68 (top and bottom), 73, 74-5, 77, 78, 79, 82, 83, 84-5, 86, 87, 90, 95, 96-7, 101, 102, 104-5, 108, 109, 113 (top), 116, 118, 119, 120, 121, 122-3, 124-5, 126 (left and right), 127, 128, 131, 134, 135, 136-7, 138-9, 140, 141, 142, 143, 153, 157, 158, 159, 175, 176, 177, 178-9, 180, 181, 182, 183, 184, 185; Alfred Hind Robinson/Hulton Archive/Getty Images 4-5; Mirrorpix 6-7, 147, 150, 153, 161, 164; ulls268239 / TopFoto 9; Hulton Archive / Stringer / Getty Images 15, 72; Universal History Archive / Getty 16, 32; Time Life Pictures / Getty Images 29; Royal Photographic Society / Getty Images 30; Barnard / Stringer / Getty Images 31; Science & Society Picture Library / Getty Images 33; David A Eastley / Alamy 36-37; English Heritage 38, 40 (top and bottom), 41, 64. 66-67, 88, 89, 103, 107, 129, 130 (top and bottom), 132 (top and bottom), 133, 152, 156, 167, 168, 172; Victoria and Albert Museum, London 44-45; Palace of Westminster Collection, WOA 3793 47; Society of Antiquaries of London 48; RCAHMS 54-55, 56; Fox Photos / Stringer / Getty Images 63, 144-5; TopFoto 69, 70-71; f8 archive / Alamy 76; Courtesy of Royal Cornwall Museum 80 (top and bottom), 81; Mary Evans Picture Library 88; Country Life 91, 92 (left and right); Courtesy of Ramsbottom Heritage Society 99; Courtesy of Manchester Libraries, Information and Archives 100; The Keasbury-Gordon Photograph Archive / Alamy 110; North Wind Picture Archives / Alamy 112; FALKENSTEINFOTO / Alamy 113 (bottom); the Llandaff Society 117; Transferred from H.M. Government War Artists' Advisory Committee, 1947 image; Manchester City Galleries 146; ulls268239 / TopFoto 148-9; PA Photos / TopFoto 163; angelroofsdotcom 170-1.